VISUAL ANALYTICS WITH TABLEAU®

VISUAL ANALYTICS WITH TABLEAU®

ALEXANDER LOTH

WILEY

Visual Analytics with Tableau®

Published by
John Wiley & Sons, Inc.
10475 Crosspoint Boulevard
Indianapolis, IN 46256
www.wiley.com

Published simultaneously in Canada

ISBN: 978-1-119-56020-3
ISBN: 978-1-119-56203-0 (ebk)
ISBN: 978-1-119-56022-7 (ebk)

Manufactured in the United States of America
V1009160 040219

For general information on our other products and services please contact our Customer Care Department within the United States at (877) 762-2974, outside the United States at (317) 572-3993 or fax (317) 572-4002.

Wiley publishes in a variety of print and electronic formats and by print-on-demand. Some material included with standard print versions of this book may not be included in e-books or in print-on-demand. If this book refers to media such as a CD or DVD that is not included in the version you purchased, you may download this material at http://booksupport.wiley.com. For more information about Wiley products, visit www.wiley.com.

Library of Congress Control Number: 2019933734

For Yue and Noah and for my parents.

About the Author

Alexander Loth is a data scientist with a background in computational nuclear research. Since 2015, he has been with Tableau Software as digital strategist. In that role, he has advised many large companies in their transformation to become data-driven organizations.

Alexander has an MBA from the Frankfurt School of Finance & Management, where he is also a lecturer for the Executive MBA programme. Prior to Tableau, he worked at the European Organization for Nuclear Research (CERN), at Capgemini, and at SAP.

A cofounder of the fintech start-up Futura Analytics, Alexander has written and spoken extensively on topics such as crypto assets, big data, machine learning, digital transformation, and business analytics.

About the Technical Editors

Florian Ramseger is a Product Specialist at Tableau Software, where he helps customers tell their data stories using Tableau Public. Prior to joining Tableau, Florian lead different data projects at the International Red Cross and the World Economic Forum. He has also worked in academia as a researcher and lecturer for macroeconomics. Florian has a BSc in Economics & Geography from University College London and a MSc in Economics & Economic History from the London School of Economics.

Mark Bradbourne has been an analytics professional since 1997. He holds a certification in Business Analytics from TDWI/ICCP and is a Certified Tableau Qualified Associate. He has been recognized as a Tableau Ambassador and works as a Tableau evangelist for KeyBank in Cleveland, Ohio. He frequently speaks at Tableau user group meetings as well as at the Tableau Fringe Festival.

Brahim Salem is a Certified Tableau Developer who has helped companies around the world understand their data better using Tableau, SQL, and Python for data visualization and manipulation. Brahim has worked in the banking, health, international development, and government sectors. He is fluent in advanced concepts such as level of detail expressions (LODs), nested LODs, custom SQL, table calculations, developing meaningful and storytelling dashboards, and data warehousing and architecture. He has extensive experience developing Tableau training materials for small and large size companies. Brahim holds an undergraduate degree in economics and a graduate degree in finance from American University.

Srilalitha Jammalamadaka is a certified Tableau specialist and data analyst helping various business clients with data visualizations. She has a master's degree in Manufacturing Engineering from Anna University, India. Recently, she has worked with Hughes Network Systems and the National Institute of Health (NIH) by using Tableau to bring out their data insights.

Credits

Associate Publisher
Jim Minatel

Editorial Manager
Pete Gaughan

Production Manager
Katie Wisor

Project Editor
Kelly Talbot

Production Editor
Athiyappan Lalith Kumar

Technical Editors
Florian Ramseger
Mark Bradbourne
Brahim Salem
Srilalitha Jammalamadaka

Copy Editor
Tiffany Taylor

Proofreader
Evelyn Wellborn

Indexer
Johnna VanHoose Dinse

Cover Designer
Wiley

Cover Image
Courtesy of Alexander Loth

Acknowledgments

I would like to thank the many people who helped make this book a reality. They provided critical feedback on initial drafts, very useful input during many conversations, and general guidance throughout the whole project. They include the people at Wiley and my colleagues at Tableau Software.

I would like to specifically mention the following names: Marcel Bickert, Michael Binzen, Mark Bradbourne, Paul Bremhorst, Richard Brünning, Andy Cotgreave, Elissa Fink, Sascha Hahn, Srilalitha Jammalamadaka, Sabine Janatschek, Janis Lasmanis, Athiyappan Lalith Kumar, Evelyn Wellborn, Jim Minatel, Florian Ramseger, Catherine Ramseger-Tan, Brahim Salem, Sophie Sparkes, Christina Schwenke, Max Sirenko, Kelly Talbot, Tiffany Taylor, Nate Vogel, Peter Vogel, and Yue Zhou-Loth.

I especially thank my family for their patience and encouragement, and particularly my wife Yue, who gave birth to our son Noah at the time of completion of this book.

Thank you very much!

Contents

Chapter 9: Sharing Insights with Colleagues and the World   205

Chapter 10: Data Preparation with Tableau Prep   221

Index   245

Foreword by Nate Vogel

Tableau was founded with a simple mission: helping people to see and understand their data. More than 15 years later, we are pursuing that same goal. A data-driven corporate culture is the key to successful digitization. Companies that involve as many employees as possible in data evaluation and promote analytical thinking are well-positioned.

Tableau gives people the power of data. We've designed our software to be flexible and capable of both helping a single person answer simple data questions and enabling thousands of people in a company to execute complex queries against massive databases.

This includes the cross-departmental use of data, because not only the amount of data, but also the number of data sources, is increasing—especially through the triumph of the cloud. This opens up completely new possibilities for analysis: With the help of professional solutions, information from different areas can be combined and integrated into a common data pool. This results in new perspectives and synergies that also make complex and strategic evaluations possible.

Tableau can help you answer questions with data. Every day, we hear stories about how Tableau helps increase sales, streamline operations, improve customer service, manage investments, assess quality and safety, investigate and treat diseases, conduct academic research, address environmental issues, and improve education!

This book will be a hands-on guide to how you can enrich your business and personal work through Alexander Loth's extensive experience with Tableau and big data. With this book, Alexander has managed to portray the use of Tableau for everyday use. In addition, he always uses practical examples to show a way to increase analytical competence.

I wish you an informative read, and I am sure that you will find numerous suggestions that can advance your company with data visualization.

Long live DATA!

Nate Vogel
Vice President, Worldwide Sales & Partner Readiness
Tableau Software

Foreword by Sophie Sparkes

We have never had more data at our fingertips than we do right now. Advances in technology are letting us capture and store more data than ever before. At the same time, the audience accessing and using data is growing ever larger. The question is, how do we find the insights within this data? And, more important, how do we communicate these insights?

We humans are a visual species. We can quickly and effectively understand complex information when it is presented in a visual form. We are also a storytelling species. We attach narratives to everything we see. So, effective data communication is a combination of images and words that explain the underlying data and analysis.

When it comes to visually analyzing data and sharing insights, Tableau is in a league of its own. Tableau's flexible drag-and-drop design lets anyone—from a single user to a company of thousands—answer their data questions. Tableau also lets you share your answers directly with your audience. Tableau truly lets people communicate with data.

This book is a hands-on guide to how you can enrich your business and personal work through Tableau. Alexander Loth's extensive experience with Tableau and big data means you are learning from the best. With this book, Alexander has successfully portrayed everyday Tableau. Additionally, his clear explanations and step-by-step practical examples guide you from the basics to more-advanced topics in a seamless fashion.

I am sure you will get a lot out of this book and wish you all the best on your data journey.

Sophie Sparkes
Community Manager
The Information Lab UK

Introduction

Visual Analytics with Tableau is intended to be a step-by-step introduction to the world of visual analytics. My hope is that you will find the provided examples to be useful for learning how to analyze your own data in Tableau.

And how to effectively communicate the new insights gained from these analyses, just like the many Tableau users with whom I have had the privilege of working in recent years.

The book should be of interest to the following audiences:

- Business professionals who make data-informed decisions on a day-to-day basis.

- Analysts and developers who create visualizations and dashboards for their organizations.

- Data scientists who want to quickly understand the data in front of them, before perhaps running more sophisticated models on it.

- Generally, anybody with access to data and with a desire to understand it.

To follow the contents of this book and to get started with Tableau, you do not need a background in mathematics or any programming experience. The book is suitable for beginners and for those who are looking for a practical introduction to the fields of data analysis and visualization.

That doesn't mean we will restrict ourselves to the basic functionality of Tableau. The first three chapters go through the essentials step by step. But this book goes deeper than that.

Building on this foundation, we will then look at more sophisticated use cases aimed at more experienced practitioners. We will cover a number of Tableau features that should be interesting even for more-advanced users.

In a few places, you will encounter short calculations and programming scripts. These are kept on the simple side, so that anybody should be able to follow their logic. Of course, more-sophisticated scenarios can be implemented in Tableau—either with Tableau's own calculated fields, which use a modern programming syntax, or via the integration of R, Python, or MATLAB. However, this is not the focus of the book. Instead of going deep into statistical programming, we will focus on the visual analytics functionality of Tableau.

STRUCTURE

This book has 10 chapters that generally build on each other. The progression of chapters is intended to support you on a continuous learning curve. Chapter 1 starts with an overview that should also help novices get a good first impression of Tableau's capabilities.

Subsequent chapters go deeper into various aspects of the visual analytics process. Chapter 2 details how to find and connect to different data sources. Chapter 3 is in some regards the heart of the book: it provides hands-on instructions for how to build assorted types of data visualizations in Tableau. I focus on the chart types that my customers and I have found most helpful in commonly encountered use cases.

Chapter 4 introduces calculated fields that allow you to add custom computations to the data. As mentioned, I have tried to make this topic accessible to as wide an audience as possible. Chapter 5 builds on Chapter 4 and covers the more-advanced, but very useful, Table Calculations and Level of Detail Calculations.

Chapter 6 looks at a very popular Tableau feature: maps. I have seen many "Eureka!" moments, when new Tableau users figured out how they can easily add their data to different types of maps. We will also talk about how to best bring in additional data without making your maps too cluttered.

Chapter 7 looks at how different statistical methods can be used to augment your visual analytics procedures to provide you with additional insights. We will cover forecasts, clusters, and trend lines, and we will also look at the integration of R, Python, and MATLAB for more advanced statistical modelling.

Chapter 8 shows how individual charts can be combined to create interactive dashboards that allow your colleagues to explore the data on their own terms. Related to that, in Chapter 9, we will look at the different options within the Tableau ecosystem for sharing your work with others: Tableau Server, Tableau Online, and Tableau Public.

Chapter 10 revisits the challenge of data preparation and data cleaning, but goes beyond what is covered in Chapter 2, by focusing on the new application Tableau Prep.

CONVENTIONS

To help you get the most from the text and keep track of what's happening, we've used a couple of conventions throughout the book.

NOTE Note boxes such as this one will provide insights into advanced Tableau functionality and working with different data structures.

TIP Tip boxes are intended to provide additional tips that should make your work with Tableau easier.

COMPANION WEBSITE

All sample data, updates, amendments, and recommended reading materials will be posted to the following website: http://www.visual-analytics.org/with-tableau.

VISUAL ANALYTICS WITH TABLEAU®

Chapter 1

Introduction and Getting Started with Tableau

Tableau was created to empower people to analyze their data regardless of the level of their technical know-how. At the core of Tableau is VizQL, an innovative visual query language that translates mouse inputs such as drag-and-drop into database queries. This allows the user to quickly find insights in their data and to share the results with others.

Crucially, it is not necessary to know what you are looking for or how you want to present your findings. Instead, with Tableau, you can immerse yourself in data. Through visual analysis, you will be able to unearth patterns and relationships in your data that you might not have known existed. In this regard, Tableau is different from other tools, which often require you to know beforehand in what form you want to display your data.

The purpose of this chapter is to introduce you to the different products that make up the Tableau application suite, the Tableau user interface, and to how Tableau processes your data. We will also introduce the sample dataset that is used throughout this book and provide a first glimpse of the possibilities that Tableau gives you for creating data visualizations.

By the end of this chapter you will be able to:

- Install Tableau on your computer.
- Identify data that is suitable for analysis.
- Create your first data visualization in Tableau.

THE ADVANTAGES OF A MODERN ANALYTICS PLATFORM

The first thing you typically do in Tableau is to connect to a dataset. The data can come from simple files, databases, data cubes, data warehouses, Hadoop clusters, or even different cloud services such as Google Analytics. Next, you interact with the Tableau interface to query your data visually and to display the results in various types of charts and maps. Then, you can collate the individual charts in a dashboard in order to put them into the right context.

Finally, depending on the product used, there are different options for communicating the results with others, from sending individual workbooks, to embedding interactive dashboards, to sharing them on social media. Tableau helps you with both the analysis as well as the communication of results, by providing capabilities such as the creation and sharing of explanatory diagrams, data stories, and interactive dashboards (see Figure 1.1).

Figure 1.1 An interactive sales dashboard. We will build this in Chapter 8.

MY PERSONAL TABLEAU STORY

I first came across Tableau in 2009, when I was writing my thesis at CERN, the European Organization for Nuclear Research in Geneva. I was exploring the landscape of available tools for the visualization and communication of data because I was not happy with the clunky, inflexible solutions that were commonly used back then.

Like most of my colleagues at CERN, I spent a lot of time aggregating data in Python, a popular universal programming language, only to then visualize it in another tool, the command-line tool GnuPlot. It was a struggle to keep all the scripts well maintained, and even small changes required a lot of time and effort.

When new data came in, the scripts had to be re-run. The resulting visualizations were, of course, static and didn't offer any interactivity to the end user. And the software packages I used had a lot of dependencies that had to be resolved every time a new version became available.

When I eventually learned about Tableau, I was amazed by the ease of use of the graphical interface and the possibility of being able to interact with my data directly.

Every time I dropped another measure or dimension onto the canvas, I got new insights from my data. What used to take me hours could now be done in minutes, and it was fun, to boot! The interactivity of the resulting dashboards and the ability to have them automatically refresh when the underlying data changed sealed the deal for me. I was a fan. I still feel as passionately about Tableau today as I did back then, and I hope to be able to impart some of that enthusiasm to the readers of this book.

THE TABLEAU APPLICATION SUITE

Some readers may have bought this book because they already have one or more Tableau products installed on their machine and would like to jump right in and learn how to use them. But for those who are not so familiar with the different Tableau products, here is a quick overview:

Tableau Desktop   Tableau Desktop is an application for Windows and Mac, appreciated by both analysts and business users. In Tableau Desktop, you can connect to flat files (such as Excel and CSV files) and save your workbooks to your local hard drive. To tap into an organization's IT infrastructure, you can also use Tableau Desktop to connect to a host of different database solutions, and you can share your workbooks via Tableau Server or the cloud-based Tableau Online.

Tableau Prep   Tableau Prep is the latest addition to the Tableau product suite and is designed to help you prepare your data before you analyze it in Tableau Desktop. The visual interface allows you to quickly merge differently formatted datasets, clean the data, and unify the level of aggregation. Tableau Prep fits seamlessly into your analysis workflow.

Tableau Server   Tableau Server is a platform for data analysis and is used by small family-run businesses and large Fortune 500 companies alike. It is intended for the organization-wide provision of data visualizations and dashboards that can be viewed in a browser and are frequently embedded into the organization's intranet.

Tableau Online   Tableau Online is a Tableau-hosted solution for storing and deploying dashboards. It provides similar functionality to Tableau Server but is a cloud-based service. No purchase and maintenance of server hardware is necessary here.

Tableau Public   Tableau Public is a hosting service for the publication of data visualizations to the web. It is used by newsrooms and bloggers but also by companies, research institutes, governmental bodies, and non-governmental organizations that aim to get their data stories into the public eye. The interactive visualizations can be viewed in the browser directly on the Tableau Public platform, or they can be embedded into blogs and websites.

Tableau Reader Tableau Reader is a free desktop application that allows you to open and interact with Tableau workbook files that have been created in Tableau Desktop. However, it is not possible to make any changes to the visualizations in Tableau Reader.

NOTE The figures throughout this book show Tableau Desktop version 2019.1, unless stated otherwise. The web-edit screen of Tableau Server and Tableau Online contains a number of features that you might recognize from Tableau Desktop. But the functionality of the browser-based products is still limited when it comes to creating new visualizations and dashboards. Therefore, I advise you to install Tableau Desktop on your machine, especially if you are still new to Tableau. The following section will provide more information about the system requirements and the installation process of Tableau Desktop.

INSTALLING TABLEAU DESKTOP

Installing Tableau Desktop is a simple process and takes only a few minutes. Therefore, this will be a very brief section.

System Requirements for Tableau Desktop

Before installing Tableau Desktop, be sure your machine meets the necessary requirements for this application. Tableau Desktop is available for Windows and Mac.

These are the official minimum requirements for a Windows installation:

- Microsoft Windows 7 or later (64-bit)
- Microsoft Server 2008 R2 or later
- Intel Pentium 4 or AMD Opteron processor or later
- 2 GB RAM
- At least 1.5 GB of free hard disk space

These are the official minimum requirements for a Mac installation:

- iMac/MacBook 2009 or later
- OS X 10.10 or later
- At least 1.5 GB of free hard disk space

Should you wish to work with large datasets, I recommend the following additional specifications:

- Latest service pack or update for your operating system
- Intel Core i3/i5/i7/i9 or AMD FX processor or later
- At least 8 GB RAM
- Solid-state drive (SSD) with at least 20 GB of free space
- Full-HD resolution (1920 × 1080 pixels) or higher with 32-bit color depth

Downloading and Installing Tableau Desktop

If you don't already have Tableau Desktop installed on your machine, use this link to download the latest trial version: https://www.tableau.com/products/desktop.

Make sure you are logged in to your machine as administrator and that you have the rights to install software on the machine. Run the installer as you normally would, given your operating system:

On a Windows Machine Open the setup (EXE) file, and accept any safety prompts from your OS.

On a Mac Open the image (DMG) file, and double-click the installation package (PKG) file to start the installation.

Follow the prompts during the setup process. Changes to the installation path or similar changes usually are not required.

Registering and Activating Tableau Desktop

Once the installation process is completed, open Tableau Desktop. A registration form will appear, which you can use to register and activate your Tableau Desktop installation using the product key.

If you do not have a product key for Tableau Desktop yet, you can test it for free for two full weeks. You will be able to use all the features of the software during this trial period.

DATA PREPARATION

Before starting any analysis, one of the key issues to consider is whether the data is in the right format.

Datasets can be structured in different ways. In most cases, datasets have one of two shapes:

- *Wide* tables, with many columns. Often these are summary tables containing aggregated measures (such as pivot tables in Excel). Here, some preprocessing of the data may be necessary.

- *Long* tables, most of the time without aggregations and with each row containing one data point.

Crosstab Reports with Wide Tables

A common mistake made by new Tableau users is attempting to connect to a fully formatted Excel report that already shows data aggregations (see Figure 1.2). Fair enough, since the claim is that you can use Tableau to visualize all sorts of data. But you will quickly realize that this won't get you very far, because you won't be able to create many different types of visualizations.

This scenario is not unusual, and it can be a stumbling block when learning how to analyze data in Tableau. Instead, the recommendation is to work with the unaggregated raw data, if you can get access to it. This will show the items broken down to the smallest units: for example, one data point per row, with each column being a unique field in the data. If that is not possible, follow the recommendations in the next section to prepare your data prior to analysis.

	A	B	C	D	E
1			Temperature Measurements		
2		Month	Morning (6:00)	Noon (12:00)	Evening (18:00)
3	Seattle				
4		April	5	17	11
5		May	9	20	15
6		June	12	25	18
7		**Average**	**8.7**	**20.7**	**14.7**
8	New York				
9		April	4	12	9
10		May	8	18	13
11		June	11	21	16
12		**Average**	**7.7**	**17**	**12.7**
13	**Average across all**		**8.2**	**18.9**	**13.7**

Figure 1.2 Formatted and aggregated report showing averages across several data points.

Preparing Your Data for Analysis

Using the example presented in the previous section, you can do the following to get the data into better shape:

- Remove the introductory text (Temperature Measurements).
- Put the hierarchical headers (Seattle, New York) in a new, separate column (Location).
- Pivot the data from the wide format, with Morning, Noon, Evening in the headers, to a *long* format, with this information about the time of day in a new column (named Time of Day). Use the full date (and time, if necessary)—for example, 01.04.2018 06:00—instead of just stating the month.
- Ensure that numbers are formatted as such and not as text.
- Remove any summary rows and columns (Average and Average Across All).
- Remove any empty rows.
- Make sure each column has a meaningful heading. For example, ensure that the date column has the heading Time Stamp and the temperature column has the title Temperature.

Long Tables Suitable for Analysis

If you followed the data-preparation steps in the previous section, you have transformed your wide crosstab into a long rows-based table that is ready for analysis in Tableau (see Figure 1.3).

	A	B	C	D
1	Location	Time Stamp	Time of Day	Temperature
2	Seattle	01.04.2018 06:00	Morning	5
3	Seattle	01.04.2018 12:00	Noon	7
4	Seattle	01.04.2018 18:00	Evening	11
5	Seattle	01.05.2018 06:00	Morning	9
6	Seattle	01.05.2018 12:00	Noon	20
7	Seattle	01.05.2018 18:00	Evening	15
8	Seattle	01.06.2018 06:00	Morning	12
9	Seattle	01.06.2018 12:00	Noon	15
10	Seattle	01.06.2018 18:00	Evening	18
11	New York	01.04.2018 06:00	Morning	4
12	New York	01.04.2018 12:00	Noon	12
13	New York	01.04.2018 18:00	Evening	9
14	New York	01.05.2018 06:00	Morning	8
15	New York	01.05.2018 12:00	Noon	18
16	New York	01.05.2018 18:00	Evening	13
17	New York	01.06.2018 06:00	Morning	11
18	New York	01.06.2018 12:00	Noon	21
19	New York	01.06.2018 18:00	Evening	16

Figure 1.3 Long table without any aggregations that is suitable for analysis in Tableau.

As you can see, every row contains exactly one temperature record with the exact time stamp. It doesn't contain any aggregations, such as averages. If you are interested in the average value, you can always calculate it in Tableau later. What's more, you can adjust the level of aggregation—the rows across which the average is to be calculated—corresponding to the questions you are asking.

THE SAMPLE DATASET

In the previous section, you saw what requirements a dataset should meet so that you can easily use it in Tableau. From here on, I will be using a sample dataset that can be found in the `Documents` directory in Tableau. It is already in the correct format and contains the sales numbers of a fictitious company called Superstore. The dataset has the following file name: `Sample - Superstore.xls`.

Finding the Dataset

The file location can vary depending on the installed version of Tableau, the operating system, and your language settings. On my Windows 10 machine, for instance, it is

```
C:\Users\<User name>\Documents\My Tableau Repository\Datasources\2019.1\en_US-EU
```

In Windows Explorer, it looks like Figure 1.4.

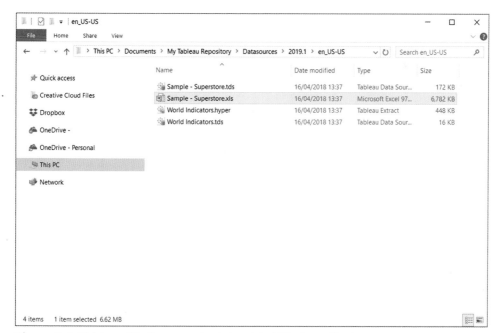

Figure 1.4 Folder with the sample dataset in Windows Explorer.

NOTE You might have noticed that Windows Explorer displays the file location differently (starting with This PC, instead of C:\).

Understanding the Data

Taking a brief glance at the data in Excel, you can see from the tabs at the bottom that the file contains three different sheets: Orders, People, and Returns (see Figure 1.5). While this dataset is a fictitious example, you could easily imagine seeing this type of sales data in a real-world setting.

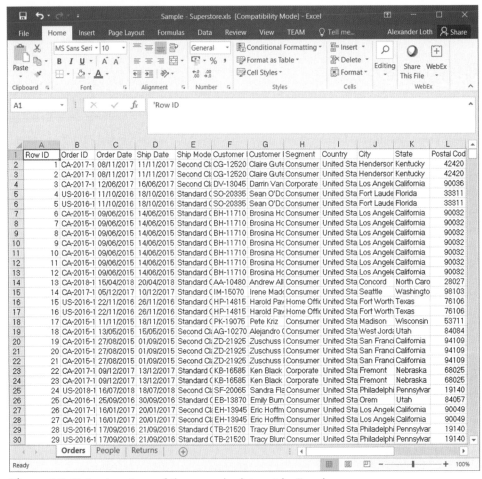

Figure 1.5 Data structure of the sample dataset in Excel.

The three tables are relational—they complement each other—and together provide information about individual sales transactions. In addition, there are no summary aggregations; each row contains one record.

Opening the Excel File Containing the Sample Dataset

When you launch Tableau Desktop, the first thing you will see is the start screen with different data types (see Figure 1.6). In the Connect panel on the left, you can select a file or a server as a data source.

Select the Microsoft Excel option under the To A File heading. Then find the Sample – Superstore.xls file in the Documents folder. Click Open to use this file as a data source in Tableau.

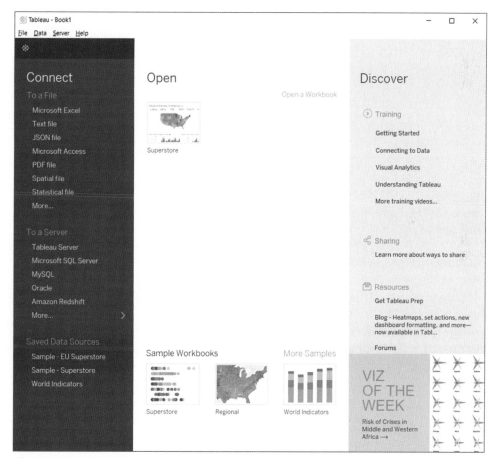

Figure 1.6 Tableau Desktop start screen.

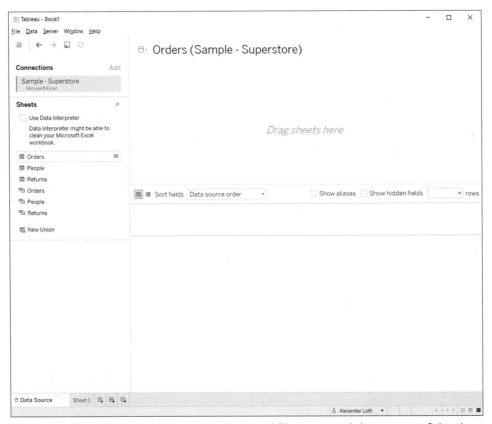

Figure 1.7 The data source view with the Excel file open and the names of the three Excel sheets shown on the left.

Tableau will then switch to the Data Source pane and, on the left-hand side, list the names of the three sheets contained in the Excel file (see Figure 1.7).

Drag and drop the `Orders` sheet onto the white space in the top half of the screen, as shown in Figure 1.8.

In the bottom half of the screen, you will now see a preview of the data. Finally, click Sheet 1 in the tabs bar at the bottom of the window, to create your first Tableau worksheet.

NOTE The examples in the following chapters of this book will all use this Superstore sample dataset, unless stated otherwise.

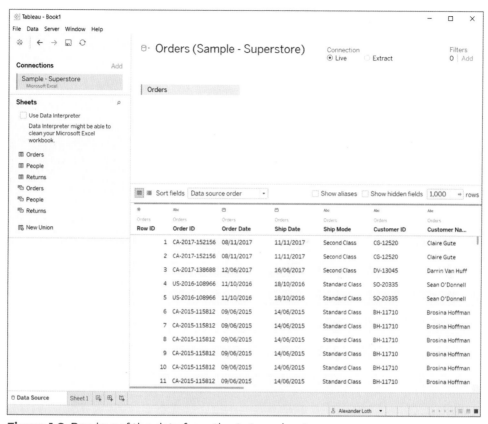

Figure 1.8 Preview of the data from the Orders sheet.

THE TABLEAU WORKSPACE

Now that you have connected to a data source and opened your first worksheet, it's time to become familiar with the Tableau interface. Figure 1.9 shows 15 numbered portions of the interface. The still-blank canvas (1), as it is called, includes the title Sheet 1 (2). On the left, you will find the Data pane (3) (more on that in the section "The Data Pane"). The tab next to it opens the Analytics pane (see Chapter 7 for more details).

In Tableau, most interactions are achieved by dragging and dropping items onto the canvas. This makes interacting with Tableau easy and intuitive. Both dimensions (4) (including hierarchical dimensions [5]) and measures (6) can be moved directly onto it. Alternatively, they can be placed on the Columns (7) and Rows (8) shelves, in order to add them to your visualization.

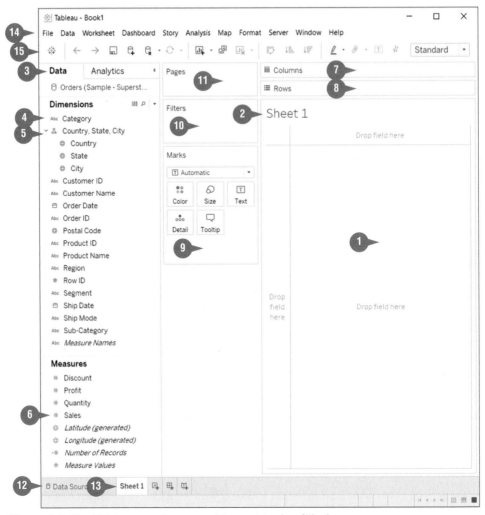

Figure 1.9 The Tableau workspace with a yet-to-be-filled canvas.

Fields from the Data pane can also be placed onto the Marks (9), Filters (10), and Pages (11) cards: for example, to change the color of marks or to only display marks for a filtered-out subset of the data. We will take a closer look at many combinations of these throughout the remainder of the book.

The tabs bar at the bottom of the screen allows you to go back to the data source editor (12) and to toggle between your different worksheets (13), each containing a single visualization. With the three buttons to the right of the tabs, you can open additional worksheets, new dashboards, and stories, respectively.

At the top of the screen, you can find the menu bar (14) (discussed in more detail in the section "The Menu Bar"). And directly under that is the toolbar (15), with three important buttons:

- **The Tableau icon:** This brings you back to the start screen, where, among other things, you can add additional data sources.
- **Undo:** This allows you to go back a step so you can safely try out different ideas. You can go back as many steps as you like.
- **Redo:** This allows you to restore any undone actions.

The Menu Bar

Even though most of the work in Tableau can be achieved by directly interacting with items using the mouse, there is also a menu bar at the top that lets you access additional features and settings. Let's take a closer look at some of the particularly useful entries:

File Menu   The File menu contains the key functions Open, Save, and Save As (see also the section "Saving, Opening, and Sharing Your Workbooks"). The Print To PDF menu item allows you to export your worksheets and dashboards as PDF files. With the Repository Location option, you can look up and change the default location for Tableau files on your machine. With Export As Version, you can create workbooks for colleagues who might still be using an older version of Tableau Desktop.

Data Menu   Here, the Insert function is especially interesting, as it presents a quick, ad hoc way to add a data table—for example, from a website. Simply select and copy the table in the original document, and click Insert in Tableau. This will add the data to your workbook as a new data source. (You will learn more about working with data sources in Chapter 2.)

Worksheet Menu   With Export, you can take your data out of Tableau by creating an image, a database file, or an Excel crosstab. Duplicate As Crosstab, on the other hand, opens a new worksheet in Tableau, showing a crosstab view of the data used in your visualization.

Dashboard Menu   Dashboard actions that add interactivity to dashboards are set up and tweaked by clicking Actions. You will learn more about filter, highlight, and URL actions in Chapter 8.

Story Menu   The Story menu entry lets you create a story from your worksheets and dashboards. In a story, content is arranged sequentially for presentation and enriched with annotations.

Analysis Menu   With this menu, you can create and edit calculated fields (see Chapter 4). Here, you will also find options for tweaking table layouts as well as for showing grand totals, forecasts, and trend lines (see Chapter 7).

Map menu   In the Map menu, you can choose between different background maps. The Offline option is particularly useful when you have no Internet connection and would like to access the built-in cartographic material. You can find more on maps in Chapter 6.

Format Menu   In this menu, you can set the font, alignment, shading, and other formatting options. In addition, you can set the overall workbook design and adjust the cell size.

Server Menu   Use this menu for sharing your dashboard via Tableau Online, Tableau Server, or Tableau Public (more on these options in Chapter 9). With the Create User Filter submenu, you can set audience-specific filters that grant specific users or user groups (which have been defined in Tableau Online or Tableau Server) access to selected subsets of the data.

Window Menu   Use the Presentation Mode option to use the full screen for your dashboard.

Help Menu   Via this menu, you have access to the Tableau online help, training videos, and sample workbooks. Use the Start Performance Recording option in the Settings And Performance submenu to analyze the processing time of your dashboard.

The Data Pane

The Data pane is divided into measures and dimensions. You control what visualizations you want to display by adding different combinations of measures and dimensions to the canvas.

Measures

SUM(Sales)

Measures are numeric variables. By adding a measure to the view, you decide which values from your dataset to visualize. By default, Tableau automatically applies an aggregation function such as SUM or AVG (the arithmetic mean) to measures. That way, you can, for instance, show the sum or the average of a sales discount across different transactions.

Measures typically (but not always) come with green symbols, which represent continuous variables.

Dimensions

`Category`

Dimensions are descriptive, categorical variables. With dimensions, you can decide how to group the aggregated values of the used measures. For instance, the sum of sales revenue (a measure) could be broken down by country, product category, or both (i.e. two different dimensions).

Typically, dimensions come with blue symbols in Tableau, which represent discrete variables.

TIP If Tableau has erroneously added a measure to the Dimensions section of the Data pane, you can simply drag it into the Measures section with the mouse, and vice versa.

WORKING WITH MEASURES AND DIMENSIONS

Now that you are familiar with the Tableau interface and know where to find measures and dimensions in the Data pane, you can finally get started with your first data visualization!

Visualizing a First Measure

Often it makes sense to start a visualization by adding a measure to the view. In the Superstore workbook, sales revenue is a good candidate.

To do this, drag the Sales measure onto the left side of the canvas, to the vertical area labeled Drop Field Here. As you can see in Figure 1.10, the area will be highlighted in green when you move a measure there.

Alternatively, you can drop the measure onto the Rows shelf above the canvas. The result is the same: you see the total sales revenue of all the records in the dataset.

TIP Do you want to see things even faster? In addition to using drag-and-drop, you can just double-click measures and dimensions in the Data pane. It does take a little getting used to, though, as Tableau automatically decides where to place the fields on the canvas, depending on the context.

Breaking Down a Measure Based on a Dimension

Having visualized your first measure, you can now break it down using one of the dimensions. You might want to learn, for example, how the sales numbers break down by product category.

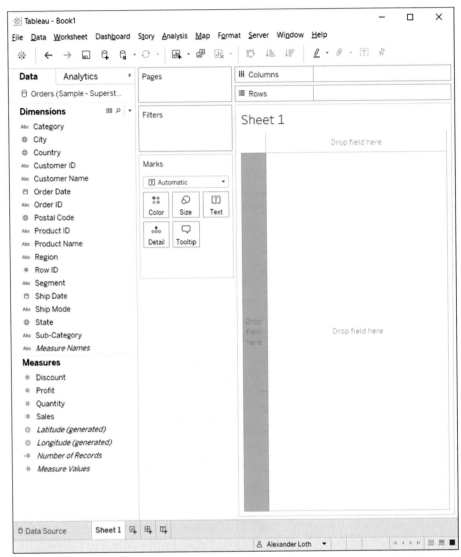

Figure 1.10 A green highlight appears when you drag a measure onto this section of the canvas.

To answer that question, hold down the mouse button and drag the Category dimension onto the upper edge of the bar chart. As you can see in Figure 1.11, a blue highlight appears as you move the dimension there.

Alternatively, you can place the dimension onto the Columns shelf above the canvas. Again, the result is the same: you see the total sales revenue broken down by product category, in accordance with the dataset.

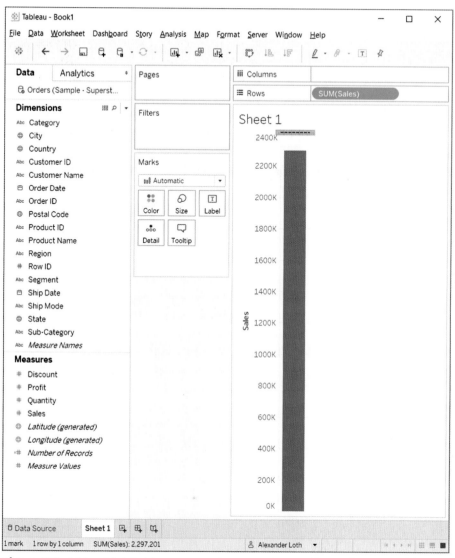

Figure 1.11 A blue highlight appears when you drag a dimension onto this part of the canvas.

WORKING WITH MARKS

After the Rows and Columns shelves, the next-most-important area is the Marks card with its various symbols. You can add dimensions and measures here, too, to further style your chart.

Among other things, you can control the color, size, form, and labeling of the marks displayed in your visualization.

Working with Color

Probably the most-used feature of the Marks card is the Color field. To try this out, drag the Segment dimension onto Color, as demonstrated in Figure 1.12.

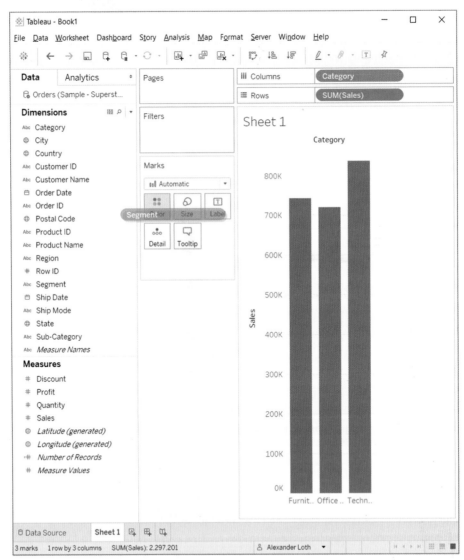

Figure 1.12 Dragging the Segment dimension onto Color.

TIP By clicking the Color field, you can choose a different color palette or, when a dimension is used, manually assign different colors to the individual items. When you place a measure onto Color, instead, you can select the colors and intervals of the color gradient.

Adding More Information to Tooltips

A *tooltip* is a little hover box that displays additional information when you point at individual marks in the visualization (see Figure 1.13). This makes your charts interactive—allowing the end user to "touch" the data—and thereby creates real added value versus static charts and PDF reports.

Drag the Profit measure onto the Tooltip field of the Marks card. Now inspect the result: view the tooltips by moving the mouse pointer over different marks in the visualization.

Tooltips add interactivity to your charts without making them more complex. They are a good place to keep secondary information that is not necessary at first glance.

TIP You can add as many measures and dimensions to a tooltip as you like. A simple click on the Tooltip field will open a text editor that allows you to change the appearance of the tooltip as required.

SAVING, OPENING, AND SHARING YOUR WORKBOOKS

Congratulations! If you have followed the previous steps, you have created your first data visualization in Tableau Desktop. Now it is time to save your work, and—if so desired—to share it with others. How to make your work available to various audiences via the different Tableau platforms (Tableau Online, Tableau Server, and Tableau Public) will be covered in Chapter 9. For now, you will save the file locally.

Saving Workbooks

Open the File menu, and click Save As. There are two different file types to choose from in the dialog box that opens:

Tableau Workbook (*.twb)   Tableau workbooks contain all the visualizations as well as the metadata. They do not, however, contain the actual data. When you share a Tableau workbook, the recipient will need to have access to the original file or database that you used.

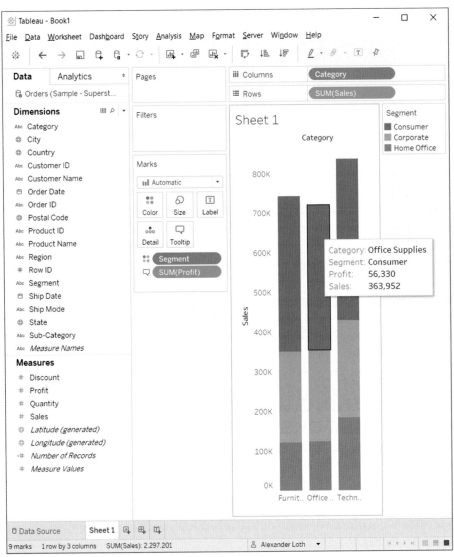

Figure 1.13 Tooltips are displayed when you point at marks.

Tableau Packaged Workbook (*.twbx) A Tableau packaged workbook, on the other hand, contains the actual data in addition to the visualizations and metadata. The data is greatly compressed, thereby reducing the overall file size. When you share a Tableau packaged workbook, the recipient will be able to open and work with your visualizations even without having access to the original data source.

Choose one of the two file types, give the file a name, and click Save.

TIP Are you on the road a lot and frequently find yourself without Wi-Fi? Make a habit of saving your work as Tableau packaged workbooks (.twbx files) so you always have your data extracts with you, even if you can't reach your database servers remotely.

Opening Workbooks

To open a previously saved workbook or packaged workbook, go to File and click Open.

Sharing Workbooks with Tableau Reader

Should you wish to share your Tableau packaged workbook with friends, acquaintances, or colleagues who do not have a Tableau Desktop license, they can open the file with the free Tableau Reader. Tableau Reader can be downloaded for Windows and Mac from the following website: https://www.tableau.com/products/reader.

NOTE In Tableau Reader, the interactivity of your visualizations is fully retained. Tooltips, for example, can be displayed as intended. However, neither the data nor the visualizations can be edited or saved in Tableau Reader.

Chapter 2

Adding Data Sources in Tableau

Often, data is not stored in just one file or database. Instead, it is frequently distributed across several databases, text files, Excel tables, or cloud services. By allowing connections to a variety of data types, Tableau makes it easy to analyze the data in such a scenario.

Tableau already supports over 50 different data connectors. You can analyze data not only from local files, including Excel, CSV, and PDF files, but also from relational databases, data cubes, Hadoop clusters, and data warehouses. Furthermore, Tableau allows access to data from cloud services such as Google Sheets, Google Analytics, Amazon Redshift, and Salesforce.

By the end of this chapter, you will be able to:

- Create connections to files and databases.
- Combine different data tables using joins and unions.
- Change the metadata and data types in your data model.

SETTING UP A DATA CONNECTOR

When you start Tableau Desktop, you see the available connectors in the Connect pane on the left side of the screen (see Figure 2.1). Different types of files are listed first; then common server types, such as Tableau Server, MySQL, and Oracle; and then the data sources to which you have recently established a connection.

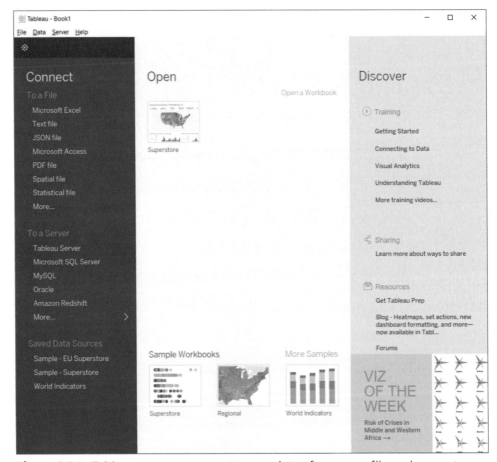

Figure 2.1 In Tableau, you can connect to a variety of common file and server types.

NOTE Contrary to how other applications commonly work, data files are not opened in Tableau. Instead, the software connects to a file or database and creates a new Tableau workbook. Tableau reads in the data, but it doesn't write back to the original file or database. This means you don't have to worry about accidentally overwriting your data. But it also means Tableau is not able to create or edit data tables. For that, you need a tool like Excel or a database system.

Connecting to a File

To analyze data that is stored in a file, simply click one of the connectors listed under To A File. The Open dialog box will show you the files on your hard drive that match the corresponding file type. All the supported files are shown in the Open dialog box (see Figure 2.2).

Click the Other Files drop-down menu to see a list of all supported file types (see Figure 2.3).

Making a selection in this menu filters the files shown in the Open dialog accordingly.

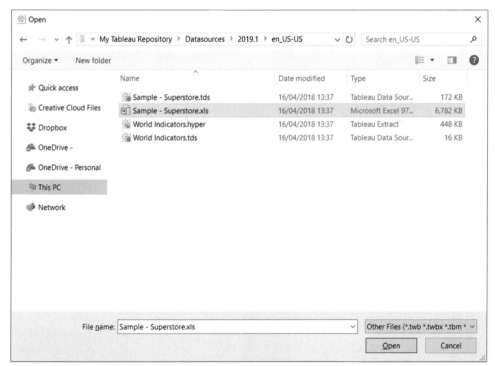

Figure 2.2 Supported file types shown in the Open dialog box.

Figure 2.3 The drop-down menu in the Open dialog shows the file types supported by Tableau.

Connecting to a Server

To analyze data located on a server, choose one of the connectors listed under To A Server. If your server type is not among the most common types listed here, click More to see a complete overview of all the available connectors that you can use (Figure 2.4).

For the databases listed here, the connectors are optimized for the specific server types. If your database technology is not on this list, you still have the option to use a generic database connector by clicking Other Databases (JDBC) or Other Databases (ODBC). However, you should only use this as a last resort, because the generic Java Database Connectivity (JDBC) and Open Database Connectivity (ODBC) interface connectors lack the optimization that the database-specific connectors offer. As a result, your analysis processes might run a little more slowly.

When you select the desired database type from the list, a window will open for you to input more details about the server. In the case of a PostgreSQL database, this looks as shown in Figure 2.5.

With most server types, you will have to provide the server name and the login details. For some of the SQL-based servers, you can also provide initial SQL commands. With databases that require SSL, you will have to select Require SSL to establish the connection.

NOTE Structured Query Language (SQL) is a database language for defining data structures and for querying and editing datasets based on those structures.

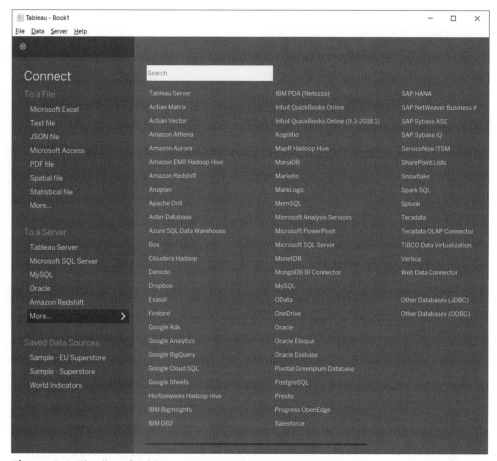

Figure 2.4 The list of Tableau-supported server connectors.

NOTE Secure Sockets Layer (SSL) is a hybrid encryption protocol for the secure transmission of data through networks.

NOTE Tableau Desktop for the Mac supports fewer server types than on a Windows machine. This is because not every database provider offers drivers for the Mac platform. However, these drivers are crucial in enabling Tableau to make a connection to the server in question.

Figure 2.5 Dialog box with connection details for a PostgreSQL database.

Connecting to a Cloud Service

Among the available connectors, you can also find several cloud services, including Dropbox, OneDrive, Salesforce, and ServiceNow. The various Google offerings that only require a free Google account are also popular:

- **Google Sheets:** A spreadsheet tool similar to Excel (see the section "Data Collection with IFTTT and Google Sheets").

- **Google Analytics:** A service for the analysis of website traffic (discussed in more detail in the section "Website Analysis with Google Analytics").

- **Google BigQuery:** A data warehouse with 10 GB of free storage space per month.

If the cloud service you require is not among the connectors listed, you still have the option to connect to it via the Web Data Connector option, which appears at the end of the list of server connectors. However, you should only use this as a last resort, because the generic web data connector (WDC) lacks the optimization that the service-specific connectors offer. As a result, your analysis processes might run a little more slowly.

Many web data connectors are open source and freely available. For instance, you might be looking for a way to connect to your Twitter data. In that case, a simple Google search for the term `Tableau WDC Twitter` should yield a suitable connector, programmed by someone in the Tableau community. In most cases, these connectors come with instructions on how to use them.

TIP Are you familiar with JavaScript and web development? In that case, you can also write your own WDC to access web-based data that is not accessible with any of the existing WDCs. For documentation, references, and examples, see this site: https://tableau.github.io/webdataconnector/.

SELECTING DATA TABLES

Having connected to a database or file, you can select one or several of its tables to build your data model. In the case of some of the connectors, including Tableau Server, Google Analytics, and the Web Data Connector, this step does not apply.

Adding a Table to a Data Model

When you work with a file-based data source, such as Excel, you will find the Sheets section in the left-hand panel. With a server-based data source, such as MySQL, PostgreSQL, or Oracle, you will see the Database and Table sections. In the latter case, you should first select the database schema that contains the tables you want to work with.

Next, select a table from Sheets (when working with files) or from Table (in the case of a database), and place it onto the blank space on the right side of the screen. Doing this with the Superstore sample dataset and the Orders sheet, you will get the view shown in Figure 2.6.

In the upper panel, you see the data model, which in this case only consists of the table named Orders. Below it is a preview of the data contained in your data model.

NOTE Not all data sources are based on relational structures. For that reason, Tableau will use a slightly modified data model for server types with cube structures (such as Microsoft Analysis Services and SAP NetWeaver Business Warehouse), as well as some of the cloud services, such as Google Analytics.

JOINS

To further build your data model and add another sheet or table, Tableau offers you the option of combining two or more tables in a relational manner. This concept is the same as that of a join in the world of SQL databases.

To create a join, pull another sheet or table onto the white space to the right of the first table. You will use the People sheet from the Superstore dataset to try this. When you release the mouse, Tableau will suggest a type of join.

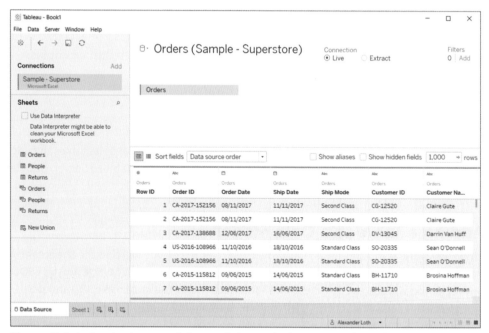

Figure 2.6 A simple data model containing only the Orders sheet from the Super-store sample dataset.

Clicking the Venn diagram symbol between the names of the two tables (Orders and People) displays several options for editing the join. By default, Tableau suggests an inner join and creates a join clause for each field that appears in both tables. In this example, Tableau suggests a join clause with the field Region, as shown in Figure 2.7, because Region appears in both tables (that is, it matches the rows of the two tables based on the values in the Region columns).

If Tableau can't find the same attribute with the same name in both tables, it will ask you to manually define a join clause. To do so, you must be familiar with the data and know which fields can be used as key attributes to join the tables. Such a relationship between two tables can also be defined with more than one join clause, and it can contain conditions other than equality (i.e. <, >, <=, >=, and <>).

In detail, the different join types have the following effects:

Inner Join

With an inner join, rows from the two tables are only joined when all the join criteria are fulfilled.

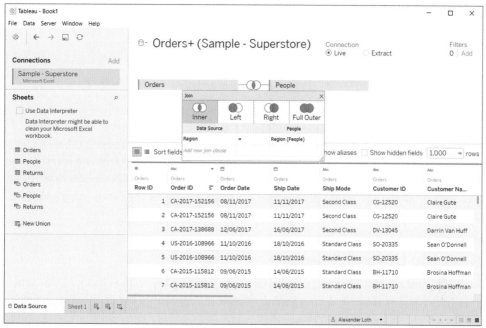

Figure 2.7 Two sheets joined based on the Region key attribute.

Left Join

Each row of the left table is used. But from the right table, rows are added only when the join criteria are fulfilled. Otherwise, the associated column entry is NULL.

Right Join

The right join works in an analogous manner to the left join, but with the rows from the right table as the starting point.

Full Outer Join

Each row is used from both the left and right tables. When rows from the left and right tables fulfill the join condition, they are matched up in the resulting table. Otherwise, the rows are added independently, and NULL values are shown in the respective columns of the other table.

TIP The sheets or tables do not necessarily have to come from the same file or from the same server. To include tables from other files or databases in your join, click Add in the Connections section of the left panel.

UNIONS

If your data is spread over several files, sheets, or tables, you can merge them by creating a union. Conceptually, this is the same as a union in SQL databases: a table can be expanded by adding rows from other sources that have the same column headers.

Drag New Union from the left panel to the work area, and a pop-up window titled Union will open. Now you can union your tables either manually or automatically using a wildcard match.

Specific Unions (Manual)

To explicitly state which sheets or tables to use in a union, stay on the window's first tab, titled Specific (Manual). Now, drag them from the left panel onto the union window (see Figure 2.8).

Click OK to create the manual union and close the dialog box.

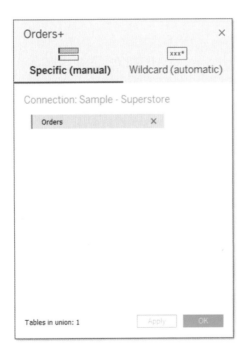

Figure 2.8 Individual sheets unioned manually.

Wildcard Unions (Automatic)

As an alternative, you can have Tableau select the sheets and tables automatically according to a search pattern. This is useful when new files or data tables are added to the directory or database over time and you don't want to manually add them to the union every time this happens.

To set this up, go to the second tab of the union dialog box: Wildcard (Automatic). Here, you can specify the folder containing the files that you want to union. Importantly, you can ensure that only certain file names or sheet names are included in the union (or that they are excluded from it).

The wildcard character ∗ can be used in the search pattern. For instance, the search term Invoices∗ will find all file names starting with Invoices (e.g. Invoices2015.xlsx, Invoices2016.xlsx, and so on). You also have the option of including subfolders and parent folders in the search. See Figure 2.9.

Click OK to create the automatic union and close the dialog box.

Figure 2.9 Files and sheets unioned automatically with a wildcard search.

TIP When creating unions of different tables, ensure that they have the same structure—for example, that they contain the same column headers. If that is not the case, the data may need some preparatory work first. This can be done in Tableau Prep, which will be discussed in Chapter 10.

DATA EXTRACTS AND LIVE CONNECTIONS

For the majority of data connectors, Tableau offers you the choice between a live connection (a direct connection to the database) and a data extract (a snapshot of the data). As shown in Figure 2.10, it is easy to switch between the two.

Live connections ensure that you are working with the latest data that is currently available in the database or file you are using. Extracting the data, on the other hand, means importing some or all of the data into Tableau's in-memory Data Engine. This is true for Tableau Desktop as well as Tableau Server. The choice between the two ways to connect to your data depends on the specific use case, the availability of the database, and the quality of the network connection.

Live Connections

By directly connecting to a database, your visualizations will always be based on the latest available data stored there. All you have to do is press F5 on your keyboard or right-click your data source, listed at the top of the Data panel, and select Refresh.

If you have a powerful database with the requisite hardware, your analyses can be conducted more quickly with a live connection. This is especially useful when you are working with large amounts of data or when you are using complex visualizations with many details.

Choosing a direct connection doesn't preclude you from extracting your data at a later point in time. Similarly, you can always switch back from an extract to

Figure 2.10 Radio buttons for switching between live connection and data extract.

a live connection by right-clicking the data source in the Data pane and selecting Extract Data.

Untethered with a Data Extract

Unlike live connections, data extracts are not updated in real time, but they have their own advantages:

Performance Improvements with Slow Data Sources   By making use of the Tableau Data Engine, an extract will relieve your database, if it receives a lot of queries or is processing a lot of transaction operations simultaneously. It is best to refresh extracts outside of peak hours. This can happen at fixed intervals, e.g. at 3:00 a.m. every night.

Incremental Extracts   Incremental refreshes of the extract reduce the time it takes to bring an extract up to date. Only new rows are added to the extracts; existing records are not extracted anew. For incremental extracts, you select an index field that is used to determine whether a row is considered to be new. Rows in the database are added only when the index is different from existing rows in the extract; the rest of the rows are disregarded in the process.

Reducing the Extract Size with Filters   Another way to make an extract faster is by using filters during the extraction process. If you don't need the entire dataset for your analysis, you can extract only the rows that are needed. In scenarios with large amounts of data, it is uncommon to extract the whole database. For instance, a database might contain data for many regions, but you only need the data for the South region.

To accomplish this, choose Extract as the connection type, and then click Edit. This will open the Extract Data window. By clicking Add, you can create a filter that will be applied to your extract (see Figure 2.11).

Added Functionality for Certain Databases   Certain databases do not support aggregations such as the median (as in the case of Access databases), and hence these are not available when using a live connection. Working with an extract will allow you to use these features, even though they are not supported by the original data source. More information about the different aggregation types will be provided in Chapter 4.

Data Accessibility   Data extracts can be saved locally and are accessible even when no connection to the original database can be established. A live connection won't let you work with your data if you can't reach the database of your data source via the local network or the Internet. Extracts are also compressed and thus much smaller than the original data tables, which makes them very portable.

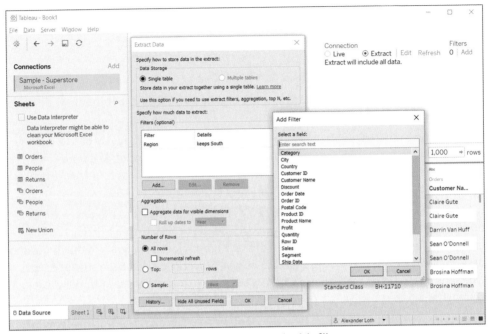

Figure 2.11 The size of an extract can be reduced with filters.

Data Protection and Data Governance

One thing you should think about when working with extracts is data protection and data governance, as well as the resulting integrity and security of your data. When you share extracts with colleagues or business partners, you want to be careful not to accidentally share any sensitive data. One option could be to limit the data with an extract filter and to aggregate it to a level that is appropriate for sharing.

If you have any doubts, it is best to work with a live connection because the rights management of your database will apply and prevent unauthorized data access.

EDITING THE MODEL'S METADATA

The metadata describes the properties of your data. If all goes well, Tableau will automatically interpret your data correctly, in some cases you will need to manually edit the metadata, especially when opening text files.

The data source's metadata can be edited directly in the preview pane in the bottom half of the screen by simply right-clicking field names in the column headers (see Figure 2.12).

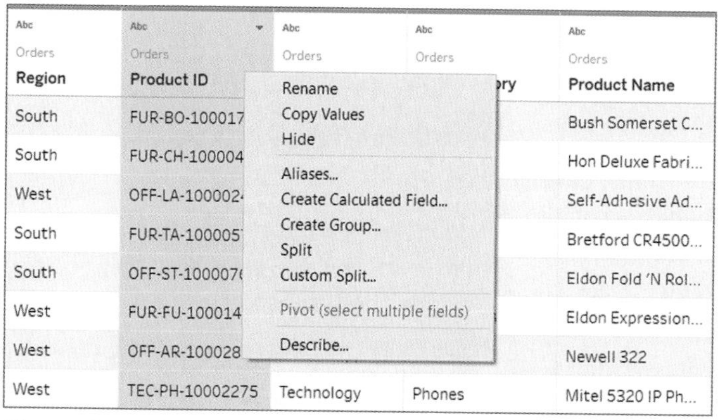

Figure 2.12 Changing the metadata in the data source editor.

You have the following options:

Renaming Fields   Click a field name with the right mouse button, and choose Rename from the context menu. Now you can define a new name for the field.

Renaming fields is especially useful with field names that were not chosen for human consumption. A field like Ord_Dt_0 might, for example, be more appropriately renamed Order Date.

Copying Values   To copy all the values of the selected field, select Copy Values from the same menu. Alternatively, to copy only certain values in the metadata grid, select these values, right-click, and then select Copy (or press Ctrl+C in Windows, or Command+C on a Mac). This feature comes in handy when you're reusing only a small portion of the data within Tableau or a spreadsheet application.

Hiding Fields   Fields that do not contain relevant information for your analysis can be excluded by selecting Hide in the same menu.

Creating Aliases   Aliases are alternate names for members in a discrete dimension. For that, select Aliases. In the Edit Aliases dialog box, under Value (Alias), select a member and enter a new name. Aliases cannot be created for continuous dimensions, dates, or measures.

Creating Calculated Fields   Choose Create Calculated Field to create a new field based on a defined logic. Creating such fields is usually done ad hoc when creating the visualization. Chapter 4 is dedicated to calculated fields.

Creating Groups   A group can combine related members in a field (e.g., combining NYC and New York City into one data point). For that, select Create Group. In the Create Group dialog box, select several members that you want to group, and then click Group. The selected members are combined into a single group.

Splitting Fields If a field contains several components that can be analyzed separately, you can split the field appropriately. To do so, select Split.

A good example in the sample dataset is the field Product ID, which is composed of three different pieces of information (e.g. FUR-BO-10000780). In this case, Tableau would split the field at the dashes, creating three new columns.

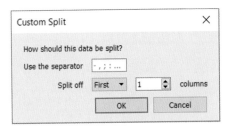

Figure 2.13 Custom splits allow you to define the separators used for the split.

Creating Custom Splits of Fields To manually define the character used for the split as well as which of the resulting columns you wish to retain, you can select Custom Split. The dialog box shown in Figure 2.13 will open.

Pivoting Data from Columns to Rows Pivoting is useful for transforming your data from a crosstab format into a columnar format. For example, suppose you have the revenue by month for five countries in five separate fields. You can pivot your data so that the country is in one field and the revenue is in another field. To pivot data, select two or more columns in the metadata grid. Then, select Pivot from the context menu. New columns called Pivot Field Names and Pivot Field Values are created and added to the data source. The new columns replace the original columns that you selected to create the pivot.

Describing Fields Chose Describe to learn more about the field's properties, such as role, type, local, and sort flags.

DATA TYPES

Each field in a data source is assigned a data type. The data type depends on the type of information stored in the field. Examples of data types include numerical values (e.g. 3.46), dates and times (10/05/2018 12:40:00 AM), and strings (South).

The data type of a field is indicated with a symbol, as shown here:

Abc

String

#

Number

T|F

Boolean

📅

Date

📅⏱

Date and Time

🌐

Geographic Entity

Changing a Field's Data Type

Occasionally, Tableau misclassifies the data type of a field. For example, it may read a date field as an integer field.

In that case, you can easily change the data type of that field by clicking the data type symbol. Simply select the appropriate data type (see Figure 2.14) in the drop-down menu.

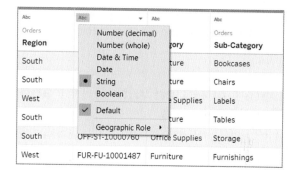

Figure 2.14 Changing the data type via a field's drop-down menu.

ADDING HIERARCHIES, CALCULATED FIELDS, AND TABLE CALCULATIONS

In Tableau, data hierarchies and calculated fields usually are not created in the data source window but are instead added as the need arises during the actual analysis process. Nevertheless, these changes to the data model will be stored as part of the data source. (If you know what calculated fields you need beforehand, you can add them by selecting Create Calculated Field in the previously mentioned context menu.)

We will cover these in more detail in the following chapters:

- Hierarchies: Chapter 3
- Calculated fields: Chapter 4
- Table calculations: Chapter 5

DATA COLLECTION

While most of the examples shown in this book are based on the Superstore sample dataset included in your Tableau installation, it can of course be more interesting to try out your newly acquired skills on real-world problems. Because not everyone who wants to learn how to use Tableau has ready access to real-world data (whether stored in a file or on a database), in this section I will show you two other strategies for obtaining interesting datasets.

Data Collection with IFTTT and Google Sheets

IFTTT (If This, Then That) is an online tool that allows you to set up automation tasks (applets) that run automatically when a certain condition is fulfilled. IFTTT applets that write their output into Google Sheets are especially useful for obtaining data. With these two tools, you can record different types of events in Google Sheets tables and thereby build your own dataset over time.

For example, you can set up IFTTT to collect all tweets published that contain a certain hashtag. To do so, you need to set up (free) user accounts with both IFTTT (ifttt.com) and Google (docs.google.com). Log in to IFTTT, and use the applet called Save Tweets Featuring Specific Content To A Spreadsheet (see Figure 2.15), which you can find here: https://ifttt.com/applets/P45PCZKW-save-tweets-featuring-specific-content-to-a-spreadsheet.

Next, you define search criteria (e.g. hashtags, users, or other content), as shown in Figure 2.16. Tweets matching these criteria will then be recorded in your spreadsheet.

Give the new spreadsheet a name (in the Spreadsheet Name field), as shown in Figure 2.17, and (optionally) define a folder in Google Drive (in the Drive Folder Path field).

Figure 2.15 IFTTT applet for collecting tweets in a Google spreadsheet.

Figure 2.16 Search criteria for IFTTT to use on new tweets coming in.

Not long after you set up everything, you should see the first tweets appear in the spreadsheet. To be able to read the data in Tableau, you will need a table header. So, add a new row at the top of the spreadsheet and give each column a name. In this example, the following descriptions will work:

- User
- Tweet
- URL
- Date

After this, the Google Sheets table should look as shown in Figure 2.18.

In Tableau, create a data source using the Google Sheets connector, and enter your Google credentials when prompted. Select the spreadsheet from the list to finalize the connection; if you work with a live connection, Tableau will have access to the latest tweets found by IFTTT (using the search criteria you defined). Finally, click the Sheet 1 tab to start visualizing the Twitter data.

Figure 2.17 Giving the spreadsheet a name.

TIP Would you like to add data on your Twitter followers as well? You can do so with a Bash script and Ruby, to further expand on the example just discussed. More details can be found in the following blog post: http://alexloth.com/2015/07/26/log-twitter-follower-stats-ifttt-google-spreadsheet/.

Website Analysis with Google Analytics

Do you have a website and want to investigate who visits it and when? Tableau has a Google Analytics connector that comes in handy in this case. Google Analytics is a free tool to capture web traffic data for your website. Once you have set up and embedded Google Analytics in your website, you can view the captured data in Tableau.

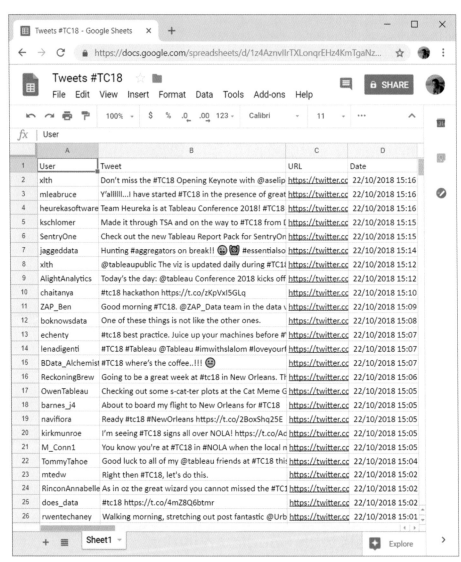

Figure 2.18 Google Sheets table with column headers.

In Tableau, set up a connection with Google Analytics, and sign in to your Google account. Instead of the usual data source editor, you will be presented with a Google Analytics–specific dialog box, as shown in Figure 2.19.

If you own several websites, choose the one you would like to analyze in Step 1. Then, in Step 2, choose the time frame that you are interested in. Finally, in Step 3, you can select up to seven dimensions and 10 measures for your analysis.

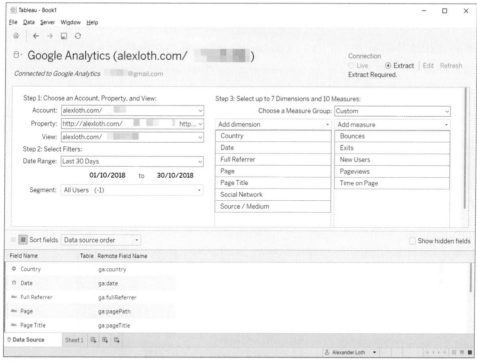

Figure 2.19 Selecting dimensions and measures when connecting to Google Analytics.

If you don't know which of the many dimensions and measures are of interest, start with the following dimensions:

- Country: Countries from which people have visited your websites.
- Date: When people have visited your website.
- Full Referrer: The origin from which people have navigated to your website (including host name and path).
- Page: The full URL for your website (including search parameters).
- Page Title: The page title of the visited website.
- Social Network: The social network, if any, from which the visitor reached your website.
- Source/Medium: The medium the visitor used to reach your website (e.g. Google search, Facebook, or a link on another website).

- Bounces: The number of times a visitor left just after viewing the page in question, without viewing any other pages of the website.

- Exits: The number of times a visitor left the website from the page in question.

- New Users: The number of visitors that visit for the first time and have not previously been to your website.

- Pageviews: The number of page views.

- Time on Page: How long visitors stay on the individual pages (in seconds).

Click Sheet 1 when you are done with the settings and are ready to start the analysis.

CHECKLIST FOR INCREASING PERFORMANCE

If your Tableau workbook is performing more slowly than expected, there are a couple of things you or your database administrator can check.

General Advice for Performance Optimization

To improve the speed of your analysis flow, pay attention to the following points:

- Use several smaller data sources to find the answers to several problems, as opposed to building a single large data source to be used for all questions.

- Avoid unnecessary joins.

- Avoid unnecessary unions.

- Use the Assume Referential Integrity option, found in the Data menu under the data source in question (see Figure 2.20). This ensures that Tableau queries the tables of the connection only when used explicitly in the view. If your data doesn't meet the referential integrity condition, your results may be inaccurate.

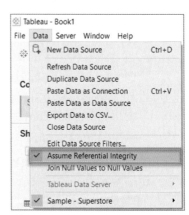

Figure 2.20 Selecting Assume Referential Integrity in the Data menu.

NOTE An example of using Assume Referential Integrity is in a query to get the values for Sales, where the SQL statement is simplified to SELECT SUM([Sales Amount]) FROM [Sales], as opposed to the longer statement SELECT SUM([Sales Amount]) FROM [Sales] S INNER JOIN [Product Catalog] P ON S.ProductID = P.ProductID.

Performance Optimization with Files and Cloud Services

When working with file formats such as Excel, PDF, and text files, or when connecting to cloud services like Google Sheets, pay attention to the following points, in addition to those mentioned in the previous section:

- Avoid joins containing several files, because the processing is very time consuming.

- With large files, use data extracts instead of live connections, because you are not working with a fast database connection (see the section "Data Extracts and Live Connections").

When creating an extract, be sure you select Single Table instead of Multiple Tables (see Figure 2.21). This results in a larger extract file, and the extract takes longer to create, but it has the advantage of making queries to the extract significantly faster.

Figure 2.21 Selecting the option Single Table in the Extract Data dialog.

Performance Optimization with Database Servers

To improve the performance of database servers such as Oracle, PostgreSQL, and Micro-soft SQL Server, pay attention to the following points:

- Define a meaningful index for your database tables.
- Add partitions to your database tables.

Chapter 3

Creating Data Visualizations

A picture is worth a thousand words.

But what exactly do you want to say with the chart you create? Keep this question in mind when you start your journey into the world of data visualization with Tableau. Useful charts are charts that have a clear purpose: they convey a message, answer questions, or provoke new questions and discussions.

There are many different ways to visually present your data in Tableau. And these graphical representations of your data can be further customized in many ways. This means, if you desire, you can create data visualizations that go beyond the standard charts you are familiar with from using other business tools. A little more diversity can also help you gain the attention of your audience and spark interest in your data, alongside the story you want to tell with it.

By the end of this chapter, you will be able to:

- Choose between simple chart types, including bar charts, scatter plots, and line charts.

- Answer comprehensive questions with more-complex chart types, including bullet graphs and waterfall charts.

- Add legends, filters, and hierarchies to your analysis.

- Follow the logic of how Tableau charts are assembled.

CHART TYPES

Independent of what type of data you want to analyze with Tableau, you should always ask yourself what chart type might work best to answer the question at hand.

The Show Me menu in Tableau, which can be found in the top-right corner of the screen, offers a variety of chart templates that you can use to create attractive data visualizations. At the end of the day, however, your creativity will be required to make a visualization truly perfect.

But there are a couple of bread-and-butter chart types among these templates that you can rely on for certain types of situations.

Scatter Plots

Scatter plots are used to show the relationship between two measures, such as revenue and profit (see the "Scatter Plots" section).

Bar Charts

Bar charts are useful to compare values of a single measure or to rank its values from the top or the bottom (see the "Bar Charts" section).

Line Charts

Line charts are commonly used to express how a measure changes over time (see the "Line Charts" section).

Highlight Tables

Highlight tables are great if you want to keep your data in a tabular format, but also visually highlight high and low points in the data (see the "Highlight Tables" section).

Heatmaps

Heat maps help you to demonstrate how a measure varies over two dimensions (see the "Heatmaps" section).

Filled Maps and Symbol Maps

Use these maps to show where something is located or if you suspect that there are geographic patterns in your data (see Chapter 6 for more details on maps).

Pie Charts

Pie charts can show parts-to-whole comparisons for individual sections. However, pie charts are a less popular chart type today than they were only a few years ago. This is due to a growing recognition that the human brain has more difficulty comparing the sizes of different pie slices than, say, the lengths of different bars. Nonetheless, there are good use cases for pie charts, including, for instance, on maps, as you will see in Chapter 6.

It is worth noting that many other (more complex) chart types, such as bullet graphs and waterfall charts, are derived from some of these more standard types of visualizations—you will see a few examples toward the end of the chapter.

NOTE Would you like to combine several different types of charts on one screen? For example, you might imagine a map to get an overview, a bar chart for more detailed information, and a line chart to see how things have changed over time.

This is achieved in Tableau with dashboards. How to put together such a collage of charts is explained in more detail in Chapter 8, which focuses entirely on dashboards.

READY, SET, SHOW ME

Tableau was developed for users who might not necessarily have any programming skills. While this is true for most things Tableau, it especially applies to the Show Me menu, which helps you achieve first results in no time. The Show Me menu integrates an assistant that makes suggestions about which chart type might fit with which data selection.

With the Show Me menu, you can also quickly build more-complex charts, such as bullet graphs (see the "Bullet Charts" section).

How Show Me Works

The Show Me assistant analyzes the combination of dimensions and measures that you have selected and suggests the chart type that will work best with your data. To try it, open the Superstore sample dataset, and go to a blank sheet. In the left-hand panel, simultaneously select the fields `Customer ID`, `Discount`, and `Sales`. On a Windows PC, you do that by holding down the Ctrl key while selecting the fields; on a Mac, you hold down the Command key.

With the three fields selected, open the Show Me menu, which can be found in the far right-hand corner of the toolbar (in case it is not yet displayed). Some of the chart types, such as maps, are not available based on your selected fields; the corresponding buttons have thus been greyed out.

Tableau highlights a recommended chart with a red border. In the case of this combination, this would be the scatter plot. However, you remain free to select any of the other chart templates, as long as the icon is not greyed out.

Scatter Plots

Now, when you click the scatter plot symbol in the Show Me menu, Tableau will automatically build the corresponding type of chart for you.

The two measures selected for Customer ID are placed on the horizontal and vertical axes, while the marks are plotted in accordance with the values of your dimension, as you can see in Figure 3.1.

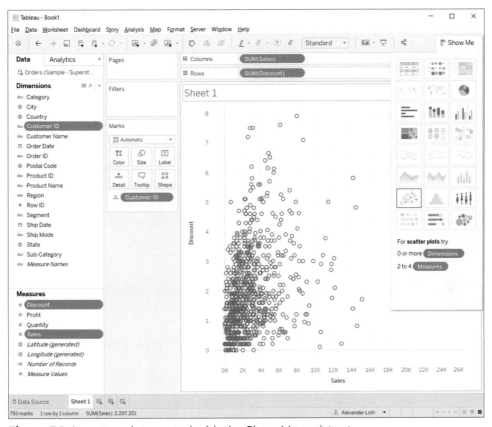

Figure 3.1 A scatter plot created with the Show Me assistant.

NOTE In this example, you include the dimension Customer ID. If you left this out and created a scatter plot without a dimension, Tableau would aggregate all available data points (the default method of aggregation is the sum). Hence, you would get exactly one mark on your scatter plot.

BAR CHARTS, LEGENDS, FILTERS, AND HIERARCHIES

The bar chart is one of the oldest and simplest chart types. It is this simplicity that makes it so appealing. Visualized as bars, measures can be easily understood without much explanation. Comparisons can readily be made: it's relatively easy to gauge the approximate difference in the lengths of two or more bars—not something that can be said for all chart types.

For that reason, bar charts lend themselves to a number of use cases and are a solid foundation for deeper investigations into the data.

Bar Charts

Bar charts are useful and can be created in Tableau with only a few clicks. In fact, starting with a blank canvas, all it takes is a double-click on a measure to get a bar chart showing the sum of the measure in question—summed over all rows in the data source. Let's try that with the measure Sales; double-click it in the Data pane, and see what happens.

Next, to break down the sum of sales breaks by product category, simply double-click Category.

If you want to add another measure to the view, such as profit, you have the option of it being in color. Let's do that: move Profit onto the Color button on the Marks card.

The bar chart will now have a color legend on the right side, as shown in Figure 3.2. Bars shaded in light blue indicate low profits, whereas those in dark blue have high profits.

If the legend is covered by the Show Me menu that you used earlier, close it by clicking the Show Me text.

TIP Do you prefer your bars horizontal, rather than vertical? By clicking the Swap Rows And Columns button (see Figure 3.2) or, even faster, by using the shortcut Ctrl+W, you can swap the axes of bar charts and many other chart types.

Hierarchies

The sample dataset contains dimensions that are in a hierarchical relationship to each other—Category and Sub-Category, for example. You can declare them to be part of a hierarchy by dragging and dropping the Sub-Category onto the Category dimension, as shown in Figure 3.3.

A plus symbol on the top-level dimension indicates the newly generated hierarchy, as shown in Figure 3.4.

Clicking the symbol allows you to break down the data to a more granular level. See Figure 3.5.

The hierarchy can be closed again by clicking the minus icon.

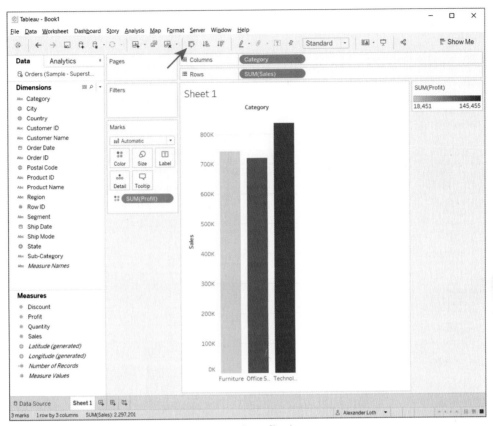

Figure 3.2 A bar chart showing sales and profits by category.

Filters

To restrict certain rows of your data to be part of your visualization, you can create filters in Tableau. To achieve this, pull a dimension or a measure onto the Filters card: for example, Segment. A dialog box will appear, allowing you to configure your filter. See Figure 3.6.

Of course, multiple values can be selected for inclusion in the view. The selection can be inverted using Exclude, meaning rows that match the selected criteria will be excluded from the visualization.

To add a control element for your filter, open the menu of the field on the filter card, and select Show Filter (the button for the menu—a small triangle icon—appears when you point at the field with the mouse).

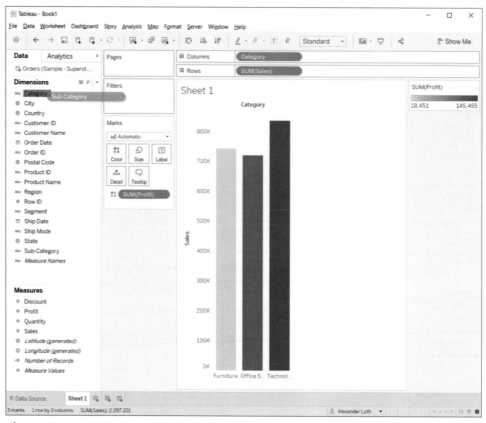

Figure 3.3 Dragging one dimension onto another to create a hierarchy.

The menu or control buttons associated with your filter should appear to the right of the visualization. See Figure 3.7.

Just as with legends, make sure the Show Me menu doesn't block the filter controls. Click the Show Me symbol to hide the menu.

Figure 3.4 Category is part of a hierarchy, as indicated by the plus symbol.

Figure 3.5 Clicking the plus symbol, you expand the hierarchy to include Sub-Category in the view.

Figure 3.6 Filter dialog box; in this example, only data rows with the segment `Consumer` are included in the visualization.

LINE CHARTS

Changes over time are often best visualized with a line chart. The dots on a line chart are typically connected with straight lines. Tableau also offers the option to use step lines and jump lines, instead.

Straight Lines

Straight lines are the most commonly used type of line charts and are suitable for showing temporal developments and trends.

Let's create a new visualization, either within a new workbook or on a new sheet within the existing workbook. Pull the measure `Sales` onto the Rows shelf. Then put the dimension `Order Date` onto the Columns shelf.

You will see a visualization showing the sum of sales by year (Figure 3.8). This is a nice chart to see when it represents data from your own business: sales revenue has increased in recent years!

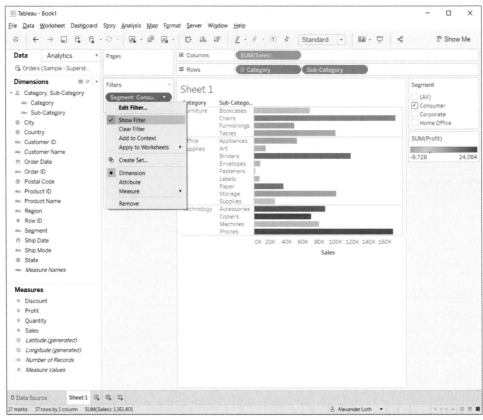

Figure 3.7 Selecting Show Filter to make the visualization more interactive.

Adjusting the Time Dimension

Fields containing dates, such as the `Order Date` dimension, are automatically treated as hierarchies by Tableau. As seen in Figure 3.9, initially the highest level of the hierarchy—years—is used.

By clicking the plus icons, you can break down the data further, first to quarter, then to month, and so on. In Figure 3.10, you see the data at the monthly level.

Should the quarter not be a meaningful unit for your analysis, you can remove it from view by dragging it off the shelf, as demonstrated in Figure 3.11.

What remains are only years and months (see Figure 3.12).

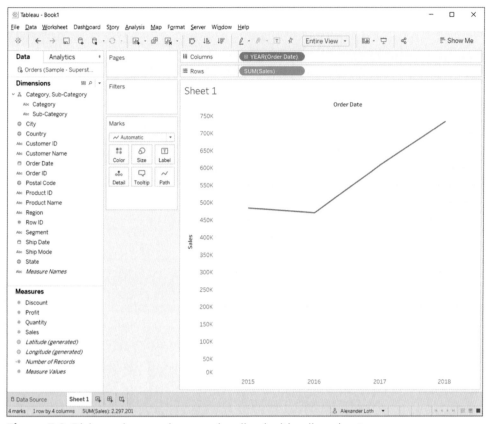

Figure 3.8 Rising sales numbers as visualized with a line chart.

Step Charts

You can use step lines to highlight the changes between two different data points. For example, this type of chart is often used to show short-term variations in interest rates.

To change your line chart to a chart with step lines, click the Path button on the Marks card. Then select the line type Step Lines, as shown in Figure 3.13.

Jump Lines

If your time-series data contains gaps, it can make sense to use the jump-lines line type, instead. One use case where this chart type is often used is the visualization of sensor data (the *Internet of Things*).

Figure 3.9 Year is the highest level of the date hierarchy.

Figure 3.10 The date hierarchy broken down to the monthly level.

Figure 3.11 Dragging the quarter off the Columns shelf.

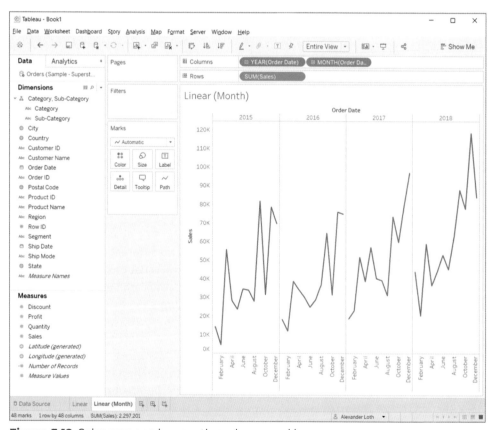

Figure 3.12 Sales revenue by month and grouped by year.

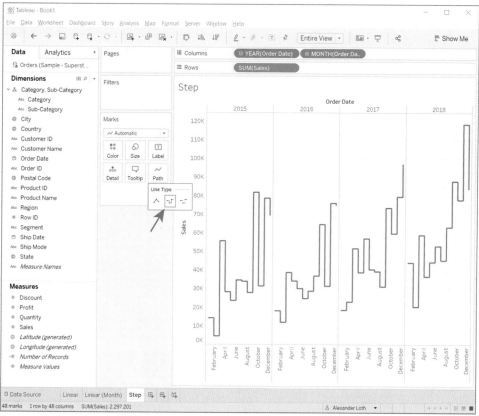

Figure 3.13 Step lines help to highlight the difference between two data points.

As with step lines, you can find the jump lines in the Path menu on the Marks card, as shown in Figure 3.14.

Continuous Date Fields

By default, Tableau treats date fields as discrete dimensions. However, you can also convert them to continuous fields. This can make sense, for example, if your data has been collected over irregular intervals, and you want to show the size of the gaps in the time series.

Move a date field to one of the shelves. Then, with a right click, open the field's context menu and select one of the options from the second block of date and time formats, such as the Week Number, as illustrated in Figure 3.15. (The upper block of date and time options contains discrete formats.)

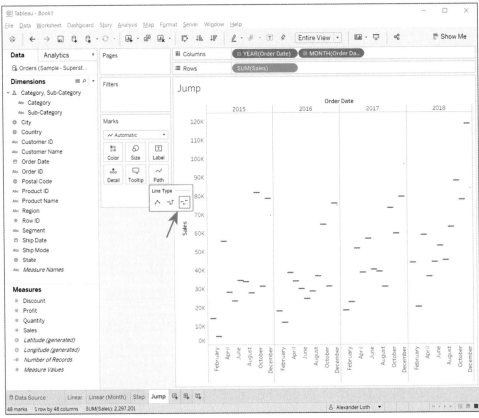

Figure 3.14 Jump lines highlight gaps in time series; this example shows sensor data.

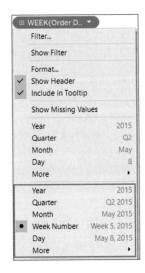

Figure 3.15 The context menu's lower block of date and time options contains continuous formats.

Continuous date fields are shown on a quantitative axis, just like most measures. In Figure 3.16, sales revenue is shown as a function of the continuous order date. You can see that after converting the Order Date field to a continuous format, it is no longer blue (discrete), but green.

TIP To change the standard property of a date field to be continuous, right-click it in the Data pane and choose Convert To Continuous. The field will now be colored green and will automatically be used as a continuous data field when added to the view. This procedure can be reversed with the menu option Convert To Discrete.

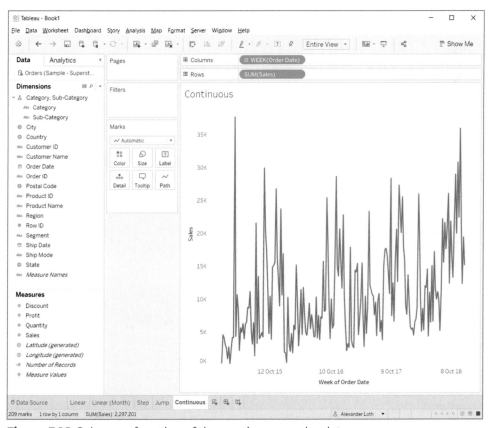

Figure 3.16 Sales as a function of the continuous order date.

HIGHLIGHT TABLES

Highlight tables are an easy-to-build alternative to classic cross tables that you might know from Excel. By adding color-coded fills, you can make it easier to spot interesting values in a sea of numbers.

Highlight tables can be a great introduction to the world of data visualization for organizations that have traditionally relied on the classic summary table to obtain insights. They are best suited for quickly identifying maximum or minimum values and other interesting data points.

To create a highlight table, you will need one or more dimensions and exactly one measure that will be used to color the table's cells. Using the sample data, let's again create a table showing sales revenue.

Step 1: Cross Tables

First, create the actual table (also called a *cross table*) by putting the Sales measure onto the text field on the Marks card, the Sub-Category dimension onto Rows, and the Order Date dimension onto the Columns shelf. For the latter, choose the hierarchy level Month from the upper block of date formats in the context menu.

The result is a cross table showing sales by subcategory over different months. See Figure 3.17. Since you are only looking at months—you didn't add Year to the view—you get the aggregate value for each month, summed up over all years.

TIP For a faster selection of the date hierarchy, add a date field to the view while holding down the right mouse button. In the step just shown, you would move Order Date onto Columns using the right mouse button. In the menu that appears when the mouse button is released, select # MONTH(Order Date) (see Figure 3.18).

Step 2: Add Color

Now, let's add some color to the view. You will color the cells according to the sales numbers of the different months. To do so, drag Sales onto the Color button on the Marks card.

Note that there are now two instances of Sales in the view: one on Text and one on Color. Your table will look as shown in Figure 3.19 and should include a color legend on the right side of the window.

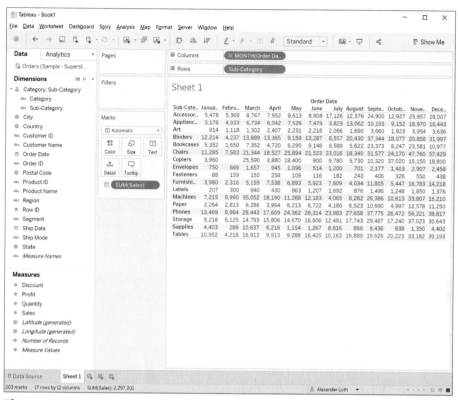

Figure 3.17 Cross table showing sales by subcategory and month.

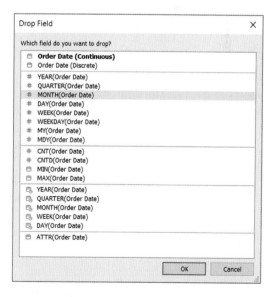

Figure 3.18 Dragging with the right mouse button.

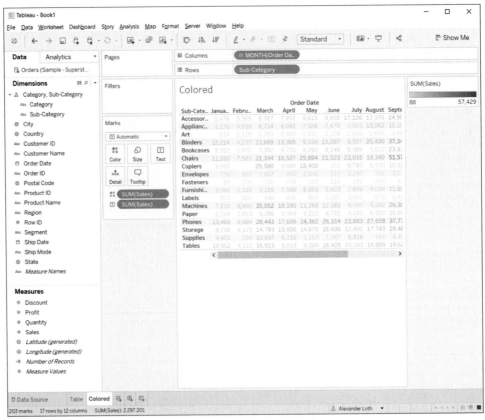

Figure 3.19 Cross table with colored text and a legend.

Step 3: Change the Mark Type

The color in the newly built table helps you to recognize the minimum and maximum values of the data more quickly than if you used a standard, black-and-white cross table. However, you can also use the white space around the figures to maximize the effect of the color.

To do that, go into the drop-down menu on the Marks card and change the mark type from Automatic to Square (as shown in Figure 3.20).

This results in a highlight table with colored cells, which makes it even easier to spot interesting values in your data; compare the result with the cross table in Figure 3.17.

TIP When creating such highlight tables, it can make sense to add a white border, to better delineate the cells. To do so, click Color on the Marks card, and select White from the Border menu.

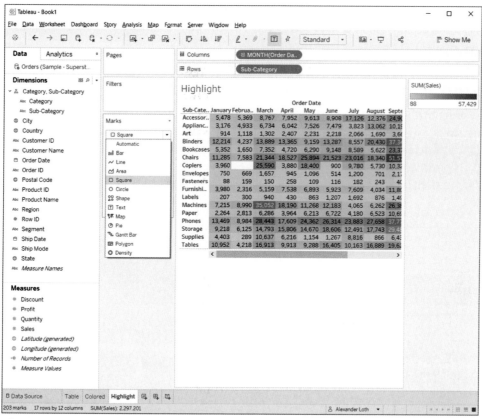

Figure 3.20 Changing the mark type to Square.

HEATMAPS

In a heatmap, the values of a measure are shown with circles of varying sizes. Higher values are assigned larger circles that are colored more intensely—hence the name heatmap. The values can be arranged in a matrix, similar to what you saw in the highlight table.

Step 1: Build the Table

To create a heatmap in Tableau, you follow the same steps you used to build a highlight table, except that the measure Sales is added to Color and Size, not Color and Text. In addition, change the mark type Circle in the drop-down menu on the Marks card.

Finally, it makes sense to give the table all the available space by selecting Entire View, instead of Standard, in the drop-down menu on the toolbar just above the canvas. See Figure 3.21.

Step 2: Choose an Interesting Color Palette

In order to do the heatmap justice and make large values appear "hot," you need a different color palette. Click the Color button on the Marks card, choose Edit Colors, and then, in the Palette menu, choose, for example, Orange-Blue Diverging.

Then, select the Reversed box in the same dialog box so that the higher values will be represented by orange circles and the lower values by blue marks (see Figure 3.22).

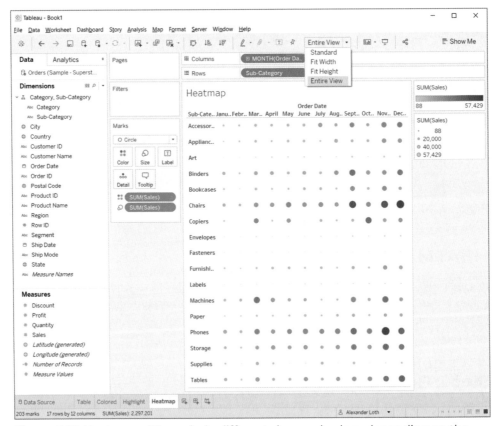

Figure 3.21 Heatmap with marks in different sizes and colors, depending on the values they represent—expanded to show the Entire View.

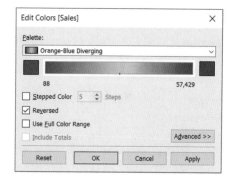

Figure 3.22 Edit Color dialog with the Orange-Blue Diverging palette and Reversed selected.

TIP Do you wonder why, in this example, we used the orange-blue palette and not the more classic red-green? While the latter palette is also available in Tableau, I discourage you from using it: approximately 9% of men and 0.8% of women suffer from red-green color blindness, meaning they have difficulty distinguishing between the two colors.

Step 3: Change the Size of Marks

If you find the circles of your heatmap too small, you can make them bigger by clicking the Size button on the Marks shelf and then moving the slider to the right. The adjusted heatmap should now look similar to the one shown in Figure 3.23.

BULLET CHARTS

A bullet chart is a variation of a bar chart. It juxtaposes two measures and shows their relation to each other; one is shown using bars, and the other using reference lines that cut across the bars. By plotting these two measures on the same axis, you can easily make a visual assessment. The differences in the two values—as indicated by the gap between the bars and the vertical reference lines—are immediately apparent. The simple, slim design of the bullet chart means a lot of information can be packed into a small space. Therefore, it also lends itself to more crowded dashboards.

For a bullet chart, you need two different measures. A common use case is to plot sales revenue and compare it with an annual or quarterly sales target.

In the sample dataset, you have `Sales`, but you don't have any target values. So, let's create a little table with sales targets for the four geographic regions of the Superstore data set. Open a blank spreadsheet in Excel, Numbers, or Google Sheets, and quickly re-create Table 3.1.

Table 3.1 Sales targets by region.

Region	Target
Central	600000
East	650000
South	500000
West	700000

Select the 10 cells in your spreadsheet, and copy the content onto the clipboard. Go back to the Tableau workbook with the Superstore data open, and press Ctrl+V to paste the data into Tableau (Command+V on a Mac); it will be added to a new data source that appears at the top of the Data pane (with the name starting with `Clipboard`). Now you can build the bullet chart you had in mind.

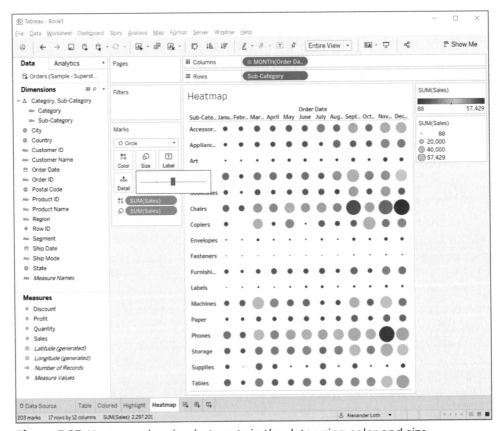

Figure 3.23 Heatmap showing hot spots in the data using color and size.

NOTE In this example, you bring in a second data source. Since the Region field is included in both data sources (the Superstore data set and the table inserted via the clipboard), Tableau automatically sets up a relationship between the two via a *blend*, as indicated by the little chain-link icon next to the Region field of the Superstore data set. That means you can work with fields from both data sources in one view.

Step 1: Side-By-Side Bars

The foundation for the bullet chart is a bar chart that shows the values for both measures side by side.

When you pasted the data into Tableau, you may have noticed that a new sheet was automatically opened, displaying the content of the table on the canvas. You can continue working with that table. First, add the Target measure to Columns. Together with Region, which is already on Rows, this gives you a bar chart showing sales revenue by region. Next, switch back to the Superstore data set by clicking Orders (Sample—Superstore) at the top of the Data pane. From the measures of that data source, pull Sales onto the Columns shelf, and place it to the right of Target. As shown in Figure 3.24, you get side-by-side bars showing both the sales target and the actual sales revenue for each region.

Step 2: Overlay the Measures

From here, you can change the chart type to a bullet chart using the Show Me assistant. Open the Show Me menu in the top-right corner, and select Bullet Graphs, as shown in Figure 3.25.

The result will be a bullet chart with the values of the two measures overlaying, instead of two separate sets of bars.

However, if you follow the instructions step by step, you may end up with Target represented by bars and the Sales values by the reference line. In a typical sales dashboard, you'd expect this to be the other way around: i.e. you want the reference lines to show the target. This can be easily fixed: right-click the horizontal axis, and select Swap Reference Line Fields. Now the measure that was used for the bars is used for the reference lines, and vice versa.

The final result should look like Figure 3.26. You can see that the regions East and West are doing great, while Central and South fall short of their sales target.

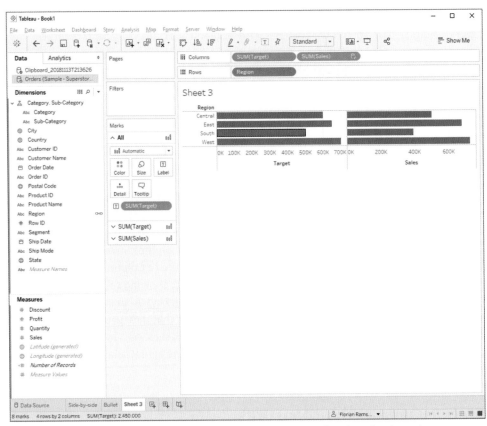

Figure 3.24 Sales revenue and sales targets next to each other, broken down by region.

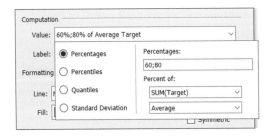

TIP You may have noticed the grey shading behind the bars of the bullet graph. These show where the numbers would reach 60% and 80% of the sales target. By right-clicking the horizontal axis and selecting Edit Reference Lines and then 60%; 80% of Average Target, you can edit the cut-off values and change the colors of these shaded fields.

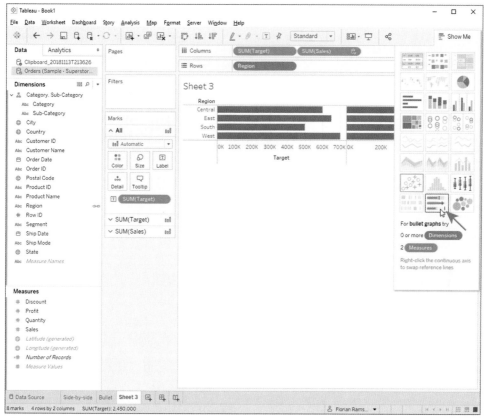

Figure 3.25 Creating a bullet chart with the help of the Show Me assistant.

CUMULATIVE SUMS WITH WATERFALL CHARTS

Waterfall charts effectively show the cumulative sum of a series of positive and negative values. The chart shows the starting value, the end value, and the incremental steps of the series. That is to say, you can see both the total change as well as the differences between consecutive values.

To create a waterfall chart, you need a dimension and a measure. From the Superstore sample data set, you can use the Sales measure and the Sub-Category dimension.

Step 1: Sorted Bar Chart

You begin by creating a bar chart and sorting the bars by the values they represent. Pull the Sales measure onto Rows and the Sub-Category dimension onto the Columns shelf.

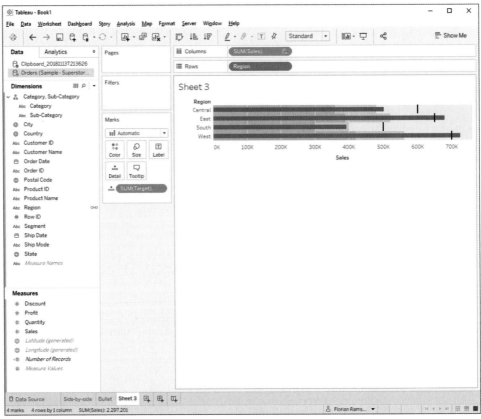

Figure 3.26 A bullet chart puts the focus on the difference between the values of two measures.

Then sort the data by sales revenue, in ascending order, by twice clicking the sort button that appears when you hover with the mouse over the vertical axis (see Figure 3.27).

Step 2: Cumulative Sum and Gantt bars

Next, right-click SUM(Sales) on the Rows shelf. In the context menu, select Quick Table Calculation and then Running Total. (We will look at Quick Table Calculations in more detail in Chapter 5.)

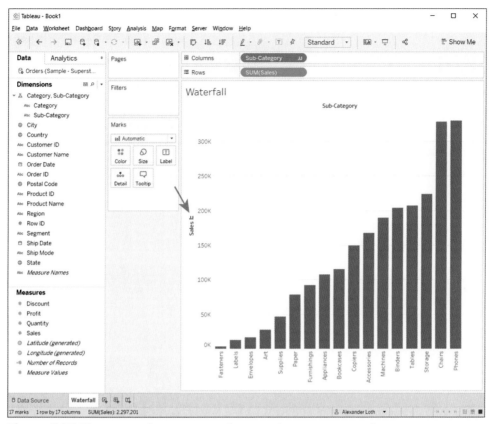

Figure 3.27 The sort option appears when you hover over an axis.

Then, change the mark type in the drop-down menu on the Marks card from Automatic to Gantt Bar. Your visualization should look like Figure 3.28.

Step 3: Calculate the Step Size

The last puzzle piece is calculating the step size between the cumulative sums. To do this, create a new calculated field by opening the menu in the Data pane (the arrow next to the Dimensions heading) and choosing the Create Calculated Field option.

Give this new field the name Sales Difference, and enter the formula –[Sales] as shown in Figure 3.29. This allows you to deduct the sales of each category from the cumulative sum—the step size. (More about calculations in Chapter 4.)

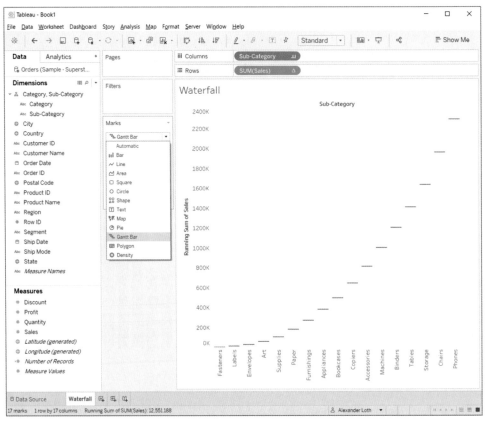

Figure 3.28 Gantt bars depicting the Running Total of sales revenue.

Figure 3.29 Calculated field with the sales difference that is needed in a waterfall chart.

Pull the newly created Sales Difference field onto the Size button on the Marks card, as shown in Figure 3.30.

If you followed the preceding steps, you have now successfully created a visualization with a more-complex chart type: a waterfall chart that shows the contributions of each subcategory to the grand total of sales.

REFLECTION: THE ANATOMY OF A TABLEAU VISUALIZATION

Even beginners can quickly create a first chart in Tableau, either using the Show Me assistant or by dragging fields onto the canvas area. The preceding pages of this chapter are

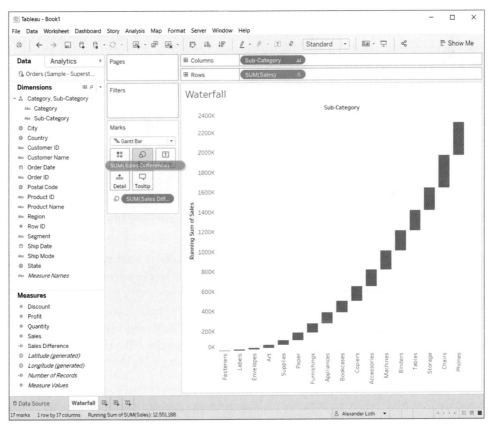

Figure 3.30 Waterfall chart showing the contribution of each subcategory to the total sum.

meant to provide step-by-step instructions to use the most common chart types in a typical business context.

However, Tableau's clever user interface allows you to go much further. More advanced users can create many other types of visualizations with only a few clicks, once they have internalized the rules by which Tableau puts together the charts from different building blocks.

You may have noticed, for example, that by default, Tableau aggregates the values of the measures used in a view. The default aggregation function is the sum of all values—but this can be changed. (We'll discuss more details of the different aggregation functions in Chapter 4.)

You can control the level of aggregation by adding dimensions to the view, to break down the data. If you don't use any dimensions, Tableau will calculate the sum over all data rows. By adding, for example Category, you instruct Tableau to calculate a separate sum for each category—that is, to sum up the values of the measure across all the data rows contained within each of the categories.

As you have seen in the examples of this chapter, dimensions and measures can be placed onto the different shelves. This happens automatically when you use the Show Me assistant. These shelves behave differently depending on whether you place a dimension or a measure on them:

Rows By placing a dimension on Rows, you break up the data. The marks will be distributed over several tabulated rows, according to the dimension used. If you add a second dimension, the result will be nested rows.

Placing a measure will give you a vertical axis, with the marks placed along it according to the sum (or another aggregation function) of the values contained by the measure. If you add a second measure, the result will be a second vertical axis.

Columns Analogous to Rows, adding a dimension to Columns will break your view into tabulated columns. Adding a measure here will give you a horizontal axis.

Marks Dimensions placed onto marks break down the data without adding more rows or columns to the view. In other words, you will get several marks (according to the dimension placed) within each cell (each combination of rows and columns). This is what happens when you place a dimension onto Color: the result is one mark for each element of the dimension, with each mark a unique color. The Size field works similarly. If you don't want to change the size or color of the marks, you can place the dimension onto the Detail field. This simply breaks up the marks without changing their appearance.

Tooltips are an exception to this rule. Placing a dimension onto a Tooltip does not break down the data further, because Tableau handles a dimension as an attribute (ATTR).

Measures generally don't influence the number of marks in a view, but they can still be placed onto the Marks card to change the size or coloring of the marks according to the measure.

To summarize, the horizontal position of your marks is controlled with Columns, and the vertical position with Rows. The number of marks (within each cell) and the styling (color, shape, and size) of the marks are influenced by placing fields onto the Marks card.

TIP You can see the data rows that make up a mark by right-clicking it, selecting View Data, and changing to the Full Data tab (see Figure 3.31).

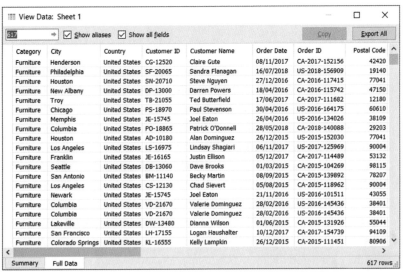

Figure 3.31 With the View Data option, you can see the data rows underlying specific marks.

After this crash course on how Tableau combines measures and dimensions to create different types of charts, it might be worthwhile to go back to the examples in this chapter or to review the different chart types on the Show Me menu. Can you follow why the measures and dimensions are placed where they are? It may take a bit of practice, but it is worth investing some time to fully understand the logic behind the charts!

Chapter 4

Aggregate Functions, Calculated Fields, and Parameters

In previous chapters, you have seen how easy it is to connect to your data from various data sources and to analyze it visually with just a few mouse clicks. With this knowledge, you are already prepared for 80% of the day-to-day use cases of Tableau.

There are, however, also those 20% of use cases that involve more complex questions and that may require the use of some more-advanced techniques, including changing the type of aggregation, creating new calculated fields, or setting up parameters.

Parameters allow you to define values external to your dataset that might have an effect on your visualization. Examples include the factors that might go into the calculation of a "what-if" scenario or search strings used to filter a text variable.

By the end of this chapter, you will be able to

- Understand when to use which type of aggregation
- Create and edit calculated fields
- Add interactivity via parameters

AGGREGATE FUNCTIONS

As you saw in the previous chapter, each individual mark in your visualization typically displays the aggregated value of a measure—aggregated across all the underlying rows in the data table associated with that mark. When working with a live connection, this aggregation can often be calculated by the database server, meaning only the aggregated values need to be sent to Tableau. If you are familiar with SQL, you will notice that several of the aggregation functions in Tableau have similar equivalents in SQL.

By default, Tableau uses Sum as the aggregation. But this is not always the most appropriate way to aggregate the data. If you need to use a different function, click the small arrow when hovering over the measure used in your view. In the menu, go to Measure (Sum), and select the aggregate function that works best for your use case (see Figure 4.1).

The types of aggregation supported by Tableau include the following:

Sum   This aggregation adds up the measure's values.

Average   This aggregation gives you the arithmetic mean of the measure's values.

Median   This aggregation gives you the median of the measure's values. For some database solutions (including MS Access, Amazon Redshift, Cloudera Hadoop, HP Vertica, IBM DB2, IBM PDA, Microsoft SQL Server, MySQL, and Teradata), the median is not available when using live connections. In such cases, you need to create an extract first when switching to this aggregate function.

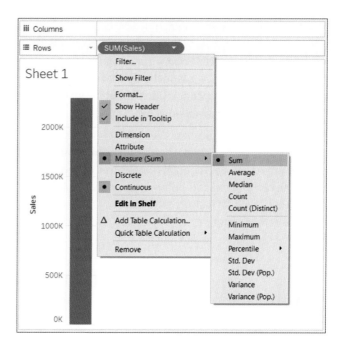

Figure 4.1 Setting the aggregate function.

Count and Count (Distinct)   These two aggregations count the occurrences of different values in two ways. Imagine that 1000 data rows underlie a specific mark in your view. Each row records a single sales transaction, and one field contains the type of product transacted (out of 30 different types of products that came up in these 1000 transactions). Using Count on the field `Product Name` will return the number of products transacted: 1000. Using Count (Distinct), on the other hand, returns the value 30; only the unique occurrences are counted. When you use a live connection to MS Access, Count (Distinct) is unavailable; you must create an extract first.

Minimum and Maximum   These aggregations return the smallest and the largest value, respectively, of a measure or a dimension.

Percentile   This aggregation returns the value for the selected percentile, chosen from the submenu: 5, 10, 25, 50, 75, 90, or 95. For some database connectors (Sybase, Oracle, Cloudera Hive, Hortonworks Hive, and EXASolution, among others), Percentile is not available for a live connection, so you first need to create an extract.

Std. Dev and Std. Dev (Pop.)   These aggregate functions return the sample standard deviation and the population standard deviation, respectively. Use the former if you are drawing conclusions about a wider population from a small sample. Std. Dev (Pop.) is the right choice when you have data for the whole population.

Variance and Variance (Pop.)   These aggregate functions return the sample variance and population variance, respectively. As with the standard deviation, use the sample variance when drawing conclusions about a wider population from a sample. Use Variance (Pop.) if your data already covers the entire population.

Dimensions and Attributes   By default, dimensions are also aggregated, because all unique values are returned when a dimension is added to a view. The values are then used to group and aggregate the measures added, as described in more detail in Chapter 3. You can prevent this behavior by choosing Attribute from a dimension's context menu. Then the information can be used for labels and tooltips, but it won't influence how the data is aggregated. (Dimension and Attribute are both located above the Measure(Sum) submenu in Figure 4.1.)

NOTE NULL values (i.e. missing values) don't flow into the calculations of the aggregate functions. While this is not an issue when you are aggregating to a sum, it does matter whether the NULL values are ignored or individually included as zeros when calculating averages, for example.

TIP To include NULL values in an aggregation as zero values, first create a calculated field with the function IFNULL([Sales], 0) (here, we're using the measure Sales as an example). This formula checks whether a value is NULL and, if so, replaces it with zero; or else returns the actual sales value. More about the use of this function can be found in the "Working with NULL Values" section.

CALCULATED FIELDS

When visualizing your data, you are not restricted to the dimensions and measures in your data source; you can also add your own calculated fields. These calculations are saved as new fields in the data model of your workbook and can be used as dimensions or measures in your visualizations.

Let's try this by adding a calculation of the profit margin to the Superstore workbook. Start by clicking the small arrow at the top of the Data pane (to the right of the Dimensions heading). In the context menu, choose the first entry, Create Calculated Field, as shown in Figure 4.2.

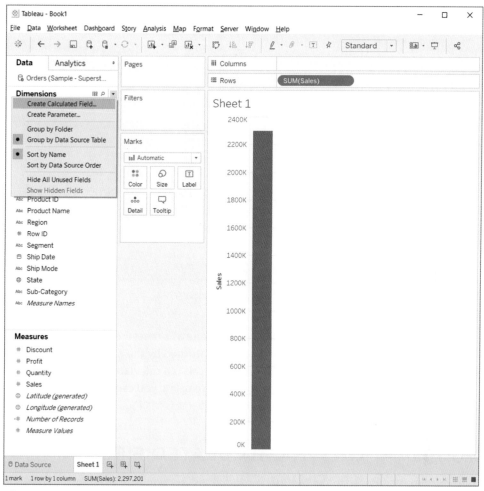

Figure 4.2 Adding a calculated field to the Data pane.

Tableau will open an empty window in the calculation editor. First, change the name of the calculated field from Calculation1 to Profit Ratio or something similar. In the empty field, add the formula for the calculation. For the profit margin, that would be

```
SUM([Profit])/SUM([Sales])
```

This simple example only uses the SUM function, but to get an overview of other allowed functions and their correct usage, expand the glossary by clicking the grey arrow at the right margin of the calculation editor (see Figure 4.3).

If the formula is correct, the valid calculation appears in the bottom-left corner of the window. Click OK to create the field and close the window.

Figure 4.3 Calculation editor with expanded glossary.

The newly created field will appear in the Data pane as a measure, as in this case, or as a dimension, depending on what kind of data is returned by the calculation. The equal sign in front of the data-type symbol indicates that this is a calculated field.

Just like the fields native to the data source you're using, you can drop calculated fields onto the canvas to create different types of charts (see Figure 4.4).

AGGREGATIONS IN CALCULATED FIELDS

The concepts introduced in the "Aggregate Functions" section play an important role when it comes to calculated fields. Let's revise the calculation of the profit margin from the previous section to understand why.

The calculated field with the formula SUM([Profit])/SUM([Sales]) returns a different result than [Profit]/[Sales], even though both are marked as "valid" in the calculation editor. The presence of the SUM operator makes a difference here.

If you were to leave out the SUM operator, Tableau would still apply a sum when the field is added to the view; as you have seen, measures are usually aggregated in Tableau. But the order of the operations would be different than you want: for each row of the data, Tableau would first calculate the ratio between profits and sales, and then sum up the results. By including SUM explicitly in the calculation, you ensure that the sum

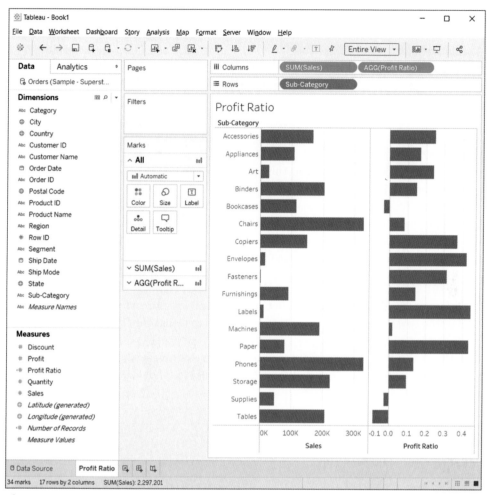

Figure 4.4 Bar chart showing both sales revenue and the calculated profit margin.

operator is applied to sales and profits separately, prior to the division of the two terms. This illustrates how important it is to understand exactly how Tableau aggregates data and to always ensure that the results returned are what you intended.

TIP In the majority of cases, it is advisable to explicitly define the aggregation in the formula for the calculated field. Make it a habit to check for missing aggregate functions, or ensure that you are happy with it being a row-level calculation.

TEXT OPERATORS

Calculated fields are not constrained to numerical calculations. Several text operators can be applied to text fields formatted as strings.

Splits

Often, a single text field contains several pieces of information. For example, the name Lisa Smith could be split into a first name and a last name. You saw in Chapter 2 how to split fields in the data source editor. This feature uses the `SPLIT` operator, which you can also use manually in a calculated field.

Let's consider the `Product Name` field in the Superstore dataset. Most of the entries contain the manufacturer name as the first word in the string: e.g. *Apple* in *Apple iPhone 5*. You can create a calculated field called `Manufacturer` to extract that information. To do so, use the following formula (see also Figure 4.5):

```
SPLIT([Product Name], " ", 1)
```

Here, you are asking Tableau to split the string `Product Name` at the spaces (as specified by the space character in quotation marks) and to return the first of the resulting segments.

Let's use this newly created field to visualize the sales revenue by manufacturer. Pull `Manufacturer` onto Rows. Then add `Sales` to Columns. You should get a bar chart like the one shown in Figure 4.6.

Figure 4.5 Calculation to split off the first word of a string.

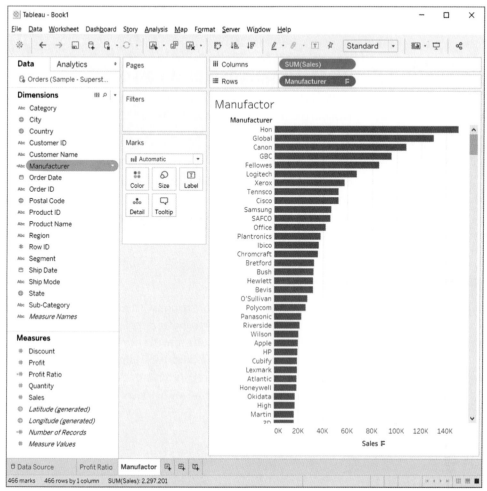

Figure 4.6 Sales revenue grouped by manufacturer, which was derived from Product Name.

Shortening Character Strings

LEFT is a text operator that returns a specified number of characters of a string, starting with the leftmost character. For instance, the following formula extracts the first two digits of the postal code:

```
LEFT(STR([Postal Code]), 2)
```

RIGHT is the analogous function to extract characters starting at the rightmost end of the string:

```
RIGHT(STR([Postal Code]), 2)
```

In both of these examples, STR is used to convert the integer Postal Code to a string, because text operators such as LEFT and RIGHT can only be applied to strings.

Converting Between Uppercase and Lowercase

At times it can be useful to change text to uppercase or lowercase, especially when the use of the case is inconsistent in the original data source. The function LOWER puts all characters of a string into lowercase:

```
LOWER([Customer Name])
```

For example, this would convert *Lisa*, *lisa*, and *LISA* all to *lisa*, and as a result reduce the number of different unique values in the field.

UPPER works in a similar manner. It converts the string into uppercase characters:

```
UPPER([Customer Name])
```

Replacing Substrings

With the REPLACE function, you can replace character strings within text fields with alternative text. It searches a field for the specified (sub)string and replaces it with your specified string of characters. This is another way to ensure consistency in your data. Think of different abbreviations that might be used in a name field: for example, PhD and Ph.D. mean the same thing to the human eye but are treated as different entities by a machine. So, to standardize the entry "Lisa Smith, PhD" as "Lisa Smith, Ph.D.," you can use the following formula:

```
REPLACE ([Customer Name], "PhD", "Ph.D.")
```

DATE FIELDS

There are several interesting date functions in Tableau, but first let's look at how Tableau breaks down dates.

Date Parts

Individual elements of a date, such as the month and year, can be referenced by date functions with the string argument date_part (see Table 4.1). It can be useful to have some familiarity with these options, because many different date functions require you to specify exactly which part of the date is affected by the calculation in question.

Table 4.1 The date parts used in Tableau.

Date part	Meaning	Permissible values
'second'	Seconds	0–59
'minute'	Minutes	0–59
'hour'	Hours	0–23 or 1am, 12pm, etc.
'day'	Days	1–31
'weekday'	Weekdays	1–7 or Monday, Tuesday, etc.
'iso–weekday'	Weekdays according to the ISO 8601 standard	1–7 or Monday, Tuesday, etc.
'week'	Week numbers	1–52
'iso–week'	Week numbers according to the ISO 8601 standard	1–52
'dayofyear'	Numbered days of the year	1–365
'month'	Months	1–12 or January, February, etc.
'quarter'	Quarters	1–4
'iso–quarter'	Quarters according to the ISO 8601 standard	1–4
'year'	Four-digit years	2019, for example
'iso–year'	Four-digit years in line with ISO-8601 standard	2019, for example

Traditional Gregorian and ISO 8601 Calendars

As you might have noticed in the previous section, you can choose between two options for some date parts. This is because different conventions exist to define these calendar units. The calendar defined by the international standard ISO 8601, which covers the format of time- and date-related data, is based on—but differs slightly from—the traditional Gregorian calendar.

The traditional Gregorian calendar defines the start of the first week of the year as 1 January, regardless of what day of the week that is. If 1 January is a Wednesday, then week 1 goes from Wednesday until the coming Tuesday; week 2 starts on the next Wednesday; and so on.

The ISO 8601 standard, on the other hand, defines week 1 of the calendar such that its start always falls on a Monday and has at least four days in January (it can start in December of the previous year). For example, should 1 January fall on a Friday, then week 1 starts on Monday, 4 January.

TIP Not all data sources support ISO 8601 date functions via a live connection. If you want to work with such date functions, you will need to create an extract, as explained in Chapter 2.

Date Calculations

The DATEADD function adds a specified time interval to a specific date; to define the interval, you specify both the date part (for example, 'day') and the length. Use cases for this formula include reference lines in time-series charts, as well as filters based on this modified date.

For example, if you assume that an order has a delivery time of three days, you can calculate the delivery time from the order date using the following formula:

```
DATEADD('day', 3, [Order Date])
```

So for the order date 12 May 2019, this function would return 15 May 2019 as the estimated delivery date.

Conversely, to find the number of days between two dates, you can use the DATEDIFF operator. DATEDIFF returns an integer value reflecting the time elapsed as measured by the specified date part (days, months, quarters, etc.). The resulting measure or dimension can be useful in various scenarios.

For example, to find out the number of days that have passed since an order was placed, you can use the following formula:

```
DATEDIFF('day', [Order Date], TODAY())
```

Here 'day' specifies that the interval is in days, [Order Date] is the start date, and the function TODAY is used to return the current date as the end date of the interval. If today is 25 April 2019 and one of the orders was placed on 10 April 2019, the calculation will return the value 15 for that particular record in the data source.

Parsing Date Parts

At times you may want to extract date parts from date fields, so you can use them individually in calculated fields.

DATEPART returns the value of the specified date part as an integer. This can be useful for calculations based on individual components of dates. Imagine, for example, that you want to report financial numbers only for the second half of the year. You can create a half-years field and use it to filter your data. To do so, you first need to know the month in which orders were placed, which is where the DATEPART function comes in:

```
DATEPART('month', [Order Date])
```

For instance, the order date 5 February 2019 will return the number 2.

This result can now be used in the formula for your new calculated field (see Listing 4.1).

LISTING 4.1

Using the DATEPART operator in a calculation to differentiate between the first and second halves of the year.

```
IF DATEPART('month', [Order Date]) < 7
  THEN '1st half of year'
  ELSE '2nd half of year'
END
```

Another useful function is the DATENAME function which returns the long-form name of a date part. Consider the following calculation, which will convert a date range into a more readable format:

```
DATENAME('month', [Start Date]) + ' to' + DATENAME('month', [End Date])
```

With a start date of 02/03/2019 and the end date 05/28/2019, you get the result "February to May."

Date Format Conversions

Dates can be stored in your dataset in different ways. Ideally, a date field is already defined as a date in the original database or Excel table. In that case, Tableau will automatically recognize it as a date, too. However, this does not necessarily have to be the case. Sometimes dates are stored as character strings, perhaps even with days, months, and years distributed over several columns, in which case they need to be merged first.

Tableau uses the default date format of your operating system, and in most cases it should recognize strings containing dates correctly as dates. But if your data source uses a different format, the dates may not be recognized or may be read incorrectly. For example, in the UK, the date 10/05/2019 typically means 10 May 2019, whereas in the United States it means 5 October 2019.

These kinds of issues can be remedied with the DATEPARSE function, which allows you to explicitly define the date format. Simply create a new calculated field with a formula similar to the following:

```
DATEPARSE ('dd/MM/yyyy', [Original Date])
```

Table 4.2 Converting different types of date formats.

String (Original Date)	DATEPARSE function	Date field (New Date)
6.3.98	DATEPARSE('d.M.yy', [Original Date])	03/06/1998
21/01/1983	DATEPARSE('dd/MM/yyyy', [Original Date])	01/21/1983
September 2018	DATEPARSE('MMMM yyyy', [Original Date])	09/01/2018
Sep 2018	DATEPARSE('MMM yyyy', [Original Date])	09/01/2018
8:42	DATEPARSE('h:m', [Original Date])	08:42
18-09-04 8:42:15	DATEPARSE('yy-MM-dd h:m:s', [Original Date])	09/04/2018 8:42:15

This function takes two arguments. The second argument ([Original Date]) refers to the original field that was not properly recognized by Tableau. Note that it must be formatted as a string; if it is already a date, you will first need to convert it to a string. The function's first argument ('dd/MM/yyyy') tells Tableau how the original date is currently formatted. In this example, it is the British way of writing dates: i.e. day followed by month, followed by year. The syntax for this argument is fairly straightforward and is best illustrated with a few more examples, such as the ones provided in Table 4.2.

The Date Field column in Table 4.2 uses the date format most commonly used in the United States. The output might look different on your machine, depending on the default date format set in your operating system.

LOGICAL FUNCTIONS IN CALCULATED FIELDS

You have already seen some examples that demonstrate how powerful calculated fields can be for creating useful measures and dimensions. But you can do even more with calculated fields. This section will introduce you to the use of application logic, including if-then statements that you may be familiar with from various programming languages.

Case Discrimination

Imagine your sales data is recorded by geographic region, as in the Superstore dataset, but you would like to report the numbers by the sales reps assigned to the different regions. This is easily done with a CASE statement.

Create a new calculated field, name it Sales Rep, and enter the formula from Listing 4.2.

LISTING 4.2

Case-discrimination logic with the CASE statement.

```
CASE [Region]
  WHEN "South" THEN "Lisa"
  WHEN "West" THEN "Peter"
  WHEN "North" THEN "Kim"
  WHEN "East" THEN "Michelle"
  ELSE "not defined"
END
```

The CASE statement in the calculated field initiates the case discrimination, in this case based on the dimension Region. The WHEN-THEN pairs define the new value to be returned for each case. For example, the output is Lisa for each record where the region is North. Should none of the stated cases apply (e.g. if a fifth region, Central, is added to the data at a later date), the ELSE statement, which is optional, ensures that the text "not defined" is displayed.

Case Discrimination with IF-THEN-ELSE Logic

IF-THEN-ELSE logic, widely known from many programming languages, can also be used in calculated fields. While many problems can be solved with the simple CASE statement we just looked at, using IF-THEN-ELSE lets you include Boolean operators and nested logic.

For instance, a manager responsible for the product subcategories Copiers, Paper, and Fasteners might be interested in comparing those numbers to those of the other subcategories. You can add a new dimension containing the newly grouped subcategories.

To do so, create a new calculated field, call it Responsibility, and enter the formula from Listing 4.3.

LISTING 4.3

Case discrimination with IF-THEN-ELSE logic.

```
IF [Sub-Category] = "Copiers"
    OR [Sub-Category] = "Fasteners"
    OR [Sub-Category] = "Paper"
  THEN "My Sub-Categories"
  ELSE "Other Sub-Categories"
END
```

According to this calculation, when (IF) the value of the dimension Sub-Category is equal to Copiers, Fasteners, or Paper, this data entry will then (THEN) be classified as My Sub-Categories. Otherwise (ELSE), the entry will be classified as Other Sub-Categories.

You can now use the newly created Responsibility field—for example, by placing it on Color to visually separate the aggregated values of the three subcategories from the rest.

TIP In Tableau, different approaches can often lead to the same outcome. In the previous example, you could achieve a similar effect by using groups. To do that, you would right-click Sub-Category in the Data pane, select Create, and then select Group. Alternatively, in a chart, you can also select the associated marks that belong to one group and click the paperclip icon in the context menu that appears. Although you can very quickly set this up in an ad hoc manner, there are drawbacks to these two methods. First, you can't use groups if you are also using aliases with a dimension. Second, for each dimension, you can have only one grouping at a time. So, the formula in Listing 4.3 is still useful to have on hand.

Case Discrimination with the IIF Function

Perhaps confusingly, there is a third way to include application logic in calculated fields: the IIF function. The IF–THEN–ELSE logic is very powerful, relatively easy to read, and simple to use with nested logic. The IIF operator provides similar results, but lends itself to more compact statements, similar to the question-mark operator in some programming languages. The downside to IIF is that more complicated, nested statements quickly become less tractable. One other difference is that IIF will carry through NULL values, as opposed to assigning them the value defined by the ELSE statement.

The IIF function requires three inputs: a test condition, followed by a THEN attribute and an ELSE attribute. If the test condition is evaluated to be true, then the value of the THEN attribute is returned. If the test condition is evaluated to be false, then the value of the ELSE attribute is returned.

A simple example is a check on whether an order is from today (the current date) or from a previous day:

```
IIF([Order Date]< TODAY(), "Old Order", "New Order")
```

If the order date is from before the current date (returned by the function TODAY), the calculated field returns Old Order; if it is not, then you get New Order.

Working with NULL Values

A more specific, but very useful, logic operator is the `IFNULL` function. It tests for NULL values, i.e. records for which no value is available, and allows you to return a different value for such records. This can be useful when these records are meant to be included in calculations as zero values. Another application would be to display a more user-friendly explanation instead of the rather cryptic NULL.

To demonstrate the second use case of the `IFNULL` function, imagine you have a Customer Email field, but it's empty for some customers because they did not provide an email address. You can create a calculated field with the following formula:

```
IFNULL([Customer Email], "Email not known")
```

When you add that field to the view, for example, you see the more informative "Email not known" label for marks associated with the empty rows, as opposed to simply NULL. Now you can quickly see all incomplete records.

PARAMETERS

Parameters enable you to capture user input on your worksheets and dashboards. The captured values can then be used in calculated fields or be displayed as reference lines in your charts. Parameter-control elements can be added to worksheets and dashboards that allow the end user to either select a value from a predefined list or freely enter a value in a text field.

Creating a Parameter and Displaying the Control Element

One potential use case for parameters is a what-if analysis. Let's try this with the Superstore data; for example, you might be interested in looking at different sales growth scenarios. To create a parameter, click the arrow next to the heading of the Data pane's Dimensions section, and choose Create Parameter, as shown in Figure 4.7.

A dialog box for configuring the new parameter appears. Let's call this parameter Factor. Set the data type to Float, define the current value as 1.1, and set the allowable values to Range. Also set the minimum value to 0.1, the maximum to 2, and the step size 0.1, as shown in Figure 4.8.

The newly created parameter will appear at the bottom of the Data pane in a new Parameters section. To add the parameter's control element to the view, open the parameter's context menu (by right-clicking it), as shown in Figure 4.9.

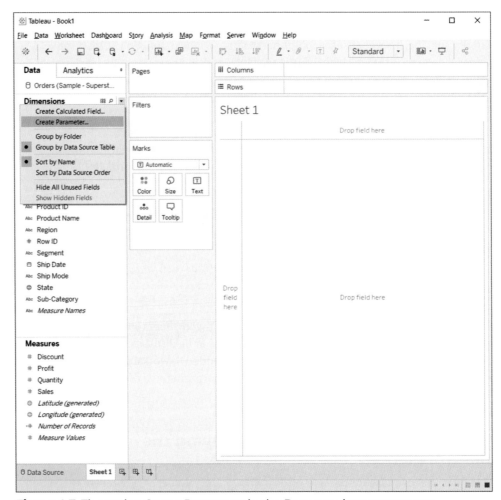

Figure 4.7 The option Create Parameter in the Data pane's context menu.

Choose the entry Show Parameter Control; it should now appear on the right side of the Tableau window.

In this case, you get a slide control labeled Factor. Using this slider, the end user can now set the value for the factor, choosing from preset values between 0.1 and 2.

Parameters in Calculated Fields

So far, the example parameter doesn't do anything. What you want to do, of course, is use the value set via the parameter control to calculate adjusted sales revenue figures:

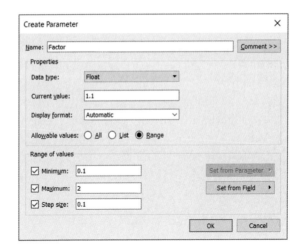

Figure 4.8 Configuring a new parameter.

e.g. what if revenue were to double? To do so, create a new calculated field with the name Adjusted Sales, and enter the following formula:

```
SUM([Sales]) * [Factor]
```

The purple formatting of the Factor field in the editor of the calculated field is an indication that it is a parameter. See Figure 4.10.

Figure 4.9 The Parameters section of the Data pane.

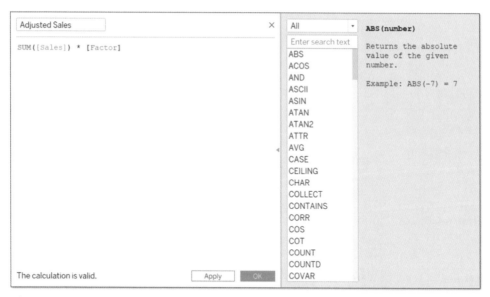

Figure 4.10 Calculated field with the Factor parameter.

Now, drag the calculated field Adjusted Sales to Columns, and add the Sub-Category dimension to Rows. If you like, you can sort the bars by their length. See Figure 4.11.

You have created a what-if analysis; the values can be adjusted by changing the growth factor in the parameter control.

SEARCHING TEXT FIELDS

I'd like to conclude this chapter with an example that draws on several previously covered concepts: parameters, calculated fields, text functions, and filters. Let's create a search box that allows you to look up customers by name, even if you don't know the whole name or the exact spelling.

Start by creating a new parameter. Call it Search, or something similar, set the data type to String, and leave the current value blank (see Figure 4.12).

After the parameter has been created, add the associated parameter control to the view. Then create a new calculated field, call it Match, and enter the following formula:

```
CONTAINS(LOWER([Customer Name]), LOWER([Search]))
```

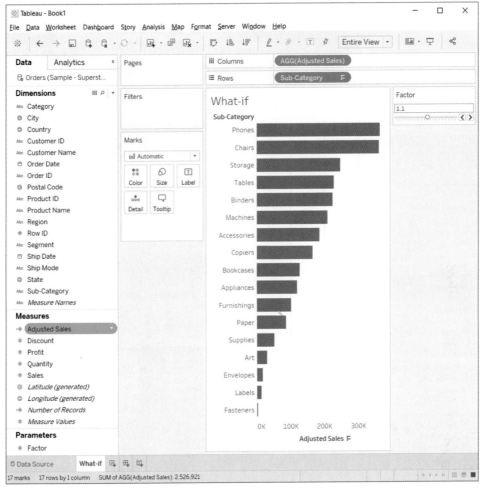

Figure 4.11 What-if analysis with a dynamic calculation based on a parameter.

Here, you use the text operator CONTAINS to test whether the current value of the parameter is contained within the customer name. To increase the hit rate, you convert both the customer name and the search text to lowercase by using the LOWER function (see also the "Converting between Uppercase and Lowercase" section).

Next, move the newly created Match field to the Filter card and choose True in the Filter dialog, as shown in Figure 4.13.

Figure 4.12 Setting up a string parameter with an empty current value.

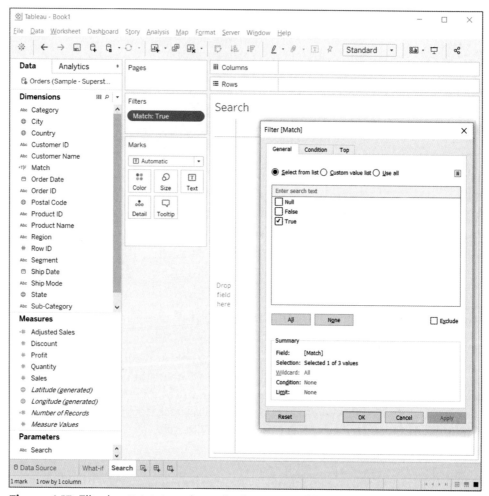

Figure 4.13 Filtering Match to only retain data rows with True.

becomes the basis of analysis, and the filters are applied first. As a result, Table Calculations are always processed in Tableau.

Order of Processing Steps

To understand the influence of processing on the calculation, it is worth taking a look at the processing steps for calculated fields, filters, and Table Calculations. This is the order in which the different processing steps are applied when creating a new chart:

1. Tableau generates a query and sends it to the data source.
2. The database processes the query. LOD statements are considered in this step.
3. Tableau generates a temporary table. Filtered-out rows are excluded from this table, and calculated fields are added as new columns.
4. It is only now that Table Calculations are processed, because they use this temporary table as a basis.
5. The chart is rendered.

Understanding the order in which the processing steps happen is important for grasping the difference between Table Calculations and other calculated fields. Table Calculations are applied last, just before Tableau renders the actual visualization. Filters are applied before Table Calculations, while normal calculated fields and LOD Calculations will be evaluated before standard filters are applied.

NOTE In addition to standard filters, there are also other filter types (context filters, extract filters, and data source filters) that are applied earlier in the process.

QUICK TABLE CALCULATIONS

Table Calculations are derived from the data shown in the view. Once you have built a first chart, you can quickly add a Table Calculation by using one of the many predefined Quick Table Calculations, including proportions, rankings, cumulative sums, and moving averages.

Setting Up a Quick Table Calculation

To demonstrate the use of Table Calculations, imagine that you want to see the cumulative sum of sales over time. Setting up a Table Calculation requires a worksheet with a first visualization. Therefore, you first create the line diagram shown in Figure 5.1 by placing Sales on Rows, Order Date (set to Continuous Months) on Columns, and Segment on Color.

Quick Table Calculations are easily applied to any measure used in the view by right-clicking the measure in question. In the context menu of Sum(Sales), choose Quick Table Calculation, as shown in Figure 5.1.

A submenu appears, listing the available Quick Table Calculations:

- Running Total

- Difference

- Percent Difference

- Percent of Total

- Rank

- Percentile

- Moving Average

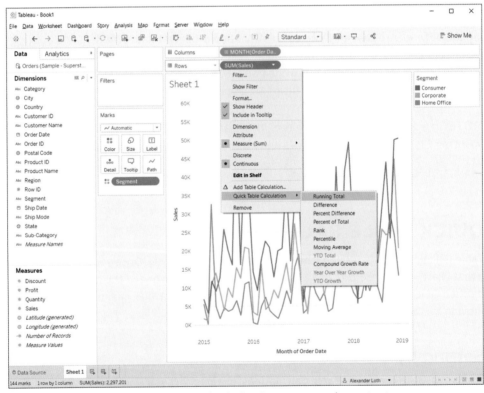

Figure 5.1 The entry Quick Table Calculation in a measure's context menu.

- YTD Total
- Compound Growth Rate
- Year Over Year Growth
- YTD Growth

Depending on the type of data used in the worksheet, some of the calculations may not be supported, and hence the associated entries might be greyed-out.

For this example, we choose Running Total. The result is a line chart showing the cumulative sum over time for each of the three segments, as shown in Figure 5.2.

TIP When a Table Calculation has been applied to a measure in the view, the delta symbol is shown to the right of the measure's name. Clicking a measure with such a symbol allows you to edit the existing Table Calculation. (See the "Editing Table Calculations" section.)

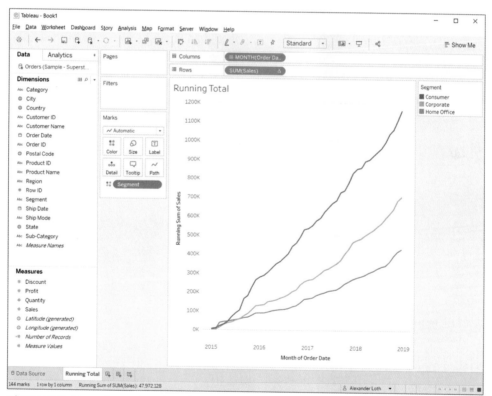

Figure 5.2 Line chart showing the running total of sales by segment.

Duplicate as Crosstab

In this book, I have so far avoided the use of crosstabs, popular as they are in many Excel reports. I find them less effective for the analysis and communication of data, as opposed to some of the charts you have already seen.

Nonetheless, I will make an exception in this chapter, because crosstabs allow me to better demonstrate how Table Calculations work. A quick way to create a crosstab is by right-clicking the tab of the current worksheet and selecting Duplicate As Crosstab (see Figure 5.3). Press Ctrl+W (Command+W on a Mac) to quickly pivot the crosstab if desired.

Editing Table Calculations

Although the Table Calculation for the running total of sales was quick to set up, Table Calculations often require paying attention to a few more settings to ensure that they

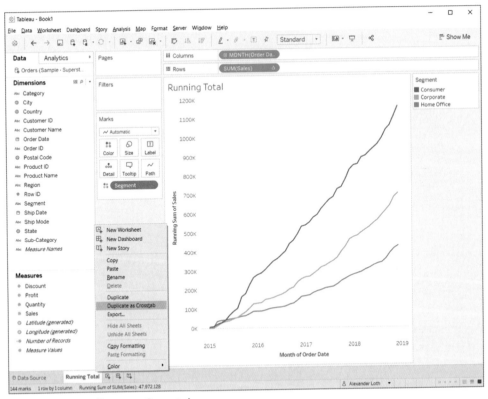

Figure 5.3 Duplicate as Crosstab.

return the intended results. To access the settings, go into the measure's context menu and choose Edit Table Calculation (see Figure 5.4).

A dialog box appears with options to configure the Table Calculation. Selecting the Show Calculation Assistance box at the bottom of the dialog box adds markup to the chart while the dialog box is open (see Figure 5.5). Depending on the chart type, you will see

- Yellow highlighting that shows the direction of calculation within a table
- Annotations that show the order of the marks within the cell of a visualization as they enter the Table Calculation

The menu at the top lists the calculation types that you have already seen. The second menu, Compute Using, is more interesting, as it allows you to define which of the dimensions you would like the calculation to run along. For that, select Specific Dimensions, and then select the dimensions along which you would like to run the calculation.

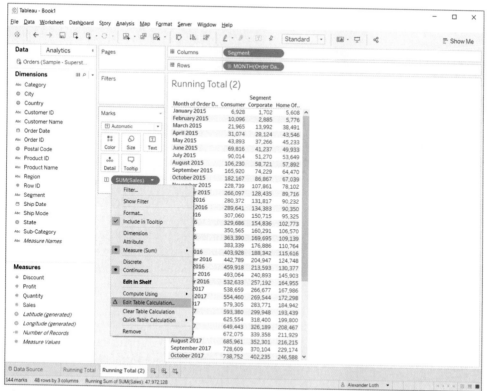

Figure 5.4 Edit Table Calculation in a measure's context menu.

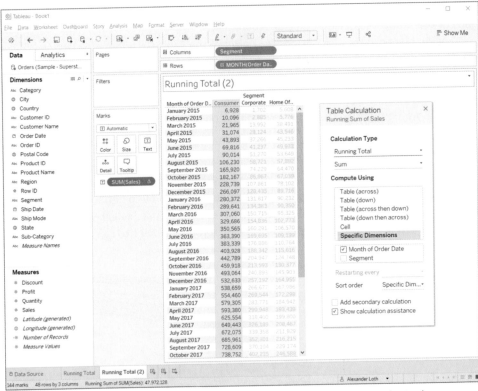

Figure 5.5 Table Calculation options with calculation assistance activated.

The calculation will be broken up by the dimensions left unselected. In this example, you want to calculate along the Month of Order Date but break up the running total by Segment, i.e. restart the computation for each new segment. Therefore, you select Month of Order Date and leave Segment unselected. Alternatively, you have the option to specify the direction of the calculation based on the temporary data table that underlies your visualization, which is made explicit here by showing the data as a crosstab, not as a chart. For instance, you can choose Table (Across) to run the calculation from left to right for each row (see Figure 5.6).

TIP Try the different options on the Compute Using menu to see how they affect the Table Calculation. Watch closely how the direction of computation changes in the crosstab, as indicated by the yellow highlighting (assuming Show Calculation Assistance is activated).

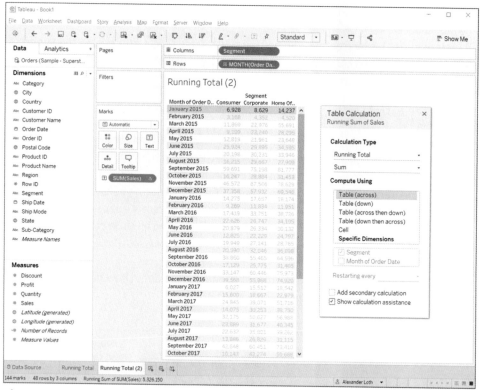

Figure 5.6 The calculation assistance (yellow shading) indicates that the Table Calculation runs from left to right.

CUSTOMIZED TABLE CALCULATIONS

You have gotten a first impression of how powerful Table Calculations can be and how quickly you can set them up. However, not all use cases are covered by the Quick Table Calculations options.

For more advanced use cases, you will need to use Table Calculation functions in calculated fields, instead. To illustrate this, let's construct a bump chart.

Bump Charts

Bump charts are a popular and effective solution for visualizing changes in rankings over time. For example, you can visualize how the ranking of product categories changes over a year. Seasonal fluctuations may also become apparent when the data is aggregated at the month level.

Let's explore this by creating a bump chart with Table Calculations using the Superstore data set. Start by creating a new calculated field. Call it Sales Rank, and enter the following formula (see also Figure 5.7):

```
RANK(SUM([Sales]))
```

As the name suggests, the Rank function in this calculated field returns the ranking of marks according to a measure—in this case, Sales. Proceed by dragging this field onto Rows, Order Date onto Columns (as discrete months), and Sub-Category onto Color.

The next important step is to define how the Table Calculation behaves in relation to the dimensions added to the view. You want to rank the different subcategories, and you want the ranking to start over for each month. To do that, go into the context menu of Sales Rank in the view, click Compute Using, and then choose Sub-Category, as shown in Figure 5.8.

For each month, you now get a ranking of products. The lines show how that ranking changes over time for individual products.

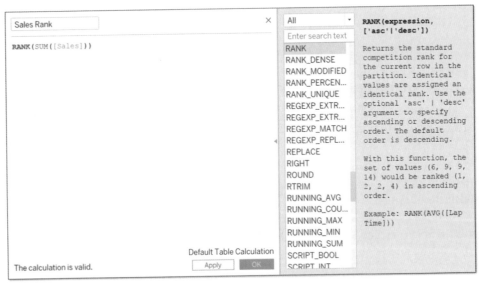

Figure 5.7 Table Calculation to compute the rank according to sales.

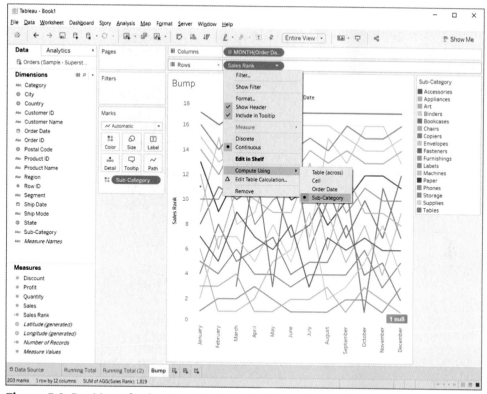

Figure 5.8 Ranking of subcategories by sales for each month.

Because it is more intuitive to have the rank values go from top (i.e. first rank) to bottom, you will invert the vertical axis to finish a basic version of the bump chart. Do that by right-clicking the axis for Sales Rank and selecting Edit Axis. Select the option for the scale to be Reversed, as shown in Figure 5.9.

The result is a bump chart showing how the different product categories fare by months of a typical year. Figure 5.10 shows clearly how the Machines product category is the top-selling product category in February and March—presumably B2B customers buy new machines early in the year—but performs worse compared to other categories during the rest of the year.

Figure 5.9 The Edit Axis dialog, with the Reversed option selected.

Dual Axis Charts

While you could easily add labels to the bends of the bump chart to show the rank for each product by month, it is common to add larger circles to such a chart in order to make the labels more readable.

To add circles to a line chart like the bump chart, you use a feature called Dual Axis. This allows you to have two charts with different mark types (lines and circles, in this case) in the same view.

Start by duplicating the Sales Rank measure on the Rows shelf. You do this by dragging Sales Rank to the free space next to it with the Ctrl key pressed. Holding the Ctrl key ensures that you get a second copy in the view. Now you see two versions of the same chart side by side. Go into the context menu of the second measure, and select Dual Axis, as shown in Figure 5.11.

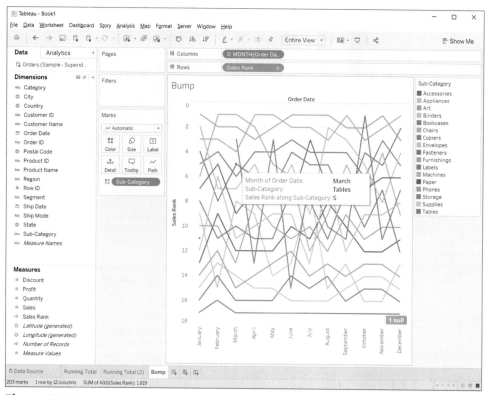

Figure 5.10 Bump chart showing the evolution of products ranked by sales, including the tooltip for Tables in the month of March.

Now the two diagrams are on top of each other, and you have two axes—one on each side of the diagram. However, the two axes are not necessarily synchronized. In fact, only the left axis has been reversed in this case. To fix that, right-click the right axis in the view, and select Synchronize Axis, as shown in Figure 5.12.

Since you effectively have two charts, you now also have two separate Marks cards that can be edited independently of one another.

Go into the lower of the two Marks cards, and change the mark type to Circle in the drop-down menu. Then drag another copy of the Sales Rank measure from the Rows shelf onto Label; as before, do that while holding the Ctrl key to get another duplicate of the measure. (In this case, you could also simply switch on labels via the button in the toolbar. But with more complex charts, it is usually advisable to define explicitly which fields you want to use for the labels.)

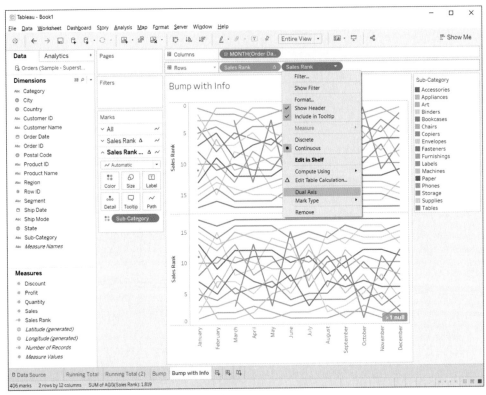

Figure 5.11 Changing to a Dual Axis plot.

You are almost there. All it needs are a few finishing touches. Click the Label button to change the font color to white. In the Alignment submenu, choose both Center and Middle. Finally, select Allow Labels To Overlap Other Marks, as shown in Figure 5.13.

The final result is a beautiful and informative bump chart that utilizes Table Calculations, dual axes, and some custom formatting.

Adjustable Moving Average

The moving average (also called the rolling average) is a popular time-series smoothing method that is often found in the field of finance as well as elsewhere.

Moving averages can be easily added as a Quick Table Calculation, but, as before, you can achieve even more sophisticated effects by manually creating them via a calculated field. For example, you can use a parameter field that will allow the end user to adjust

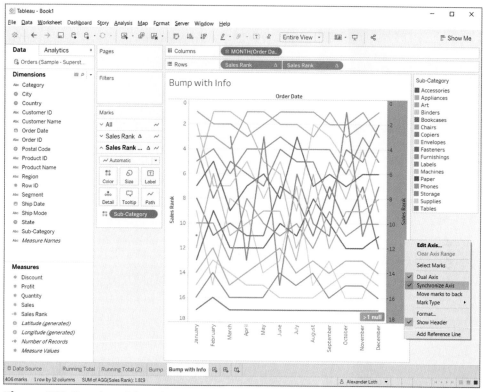

Figure 5.12 Synchronizing the axes.

the window size of the moving-average function. This way, they can select how closely the line should follow the variations in the original time series data.

Let's try this with the Sales measure. Start out with a basic line chart, created by placing Sales on Rows and adding the Order Date (as continuous months) to Columns. Next, create a new parameter by going into the menu of the Data pane and selecting Create Parameter, as shown in Figure 5.14.

Give the new parameter a name, such as Time Period, and change Data Type to Integer. Also set Allowable Values to Range, Current Value to 10, Minimum to 2, Maximum to 30, and Step Size to 1 (see Figure 5.15).

After you close the settings dialog, find the new parameter in the Data pane, and choose Show Parameter Control from its context menu.

Then create a new calculated field, call it Moving Average, and add the following formula (see also Figure 5.16):

```
WINDOW_AVG(SUM([Sales]), -[Time Period], 0)
```

Chapter 5: Table Calculations and Level of Detail Calculations   **119**

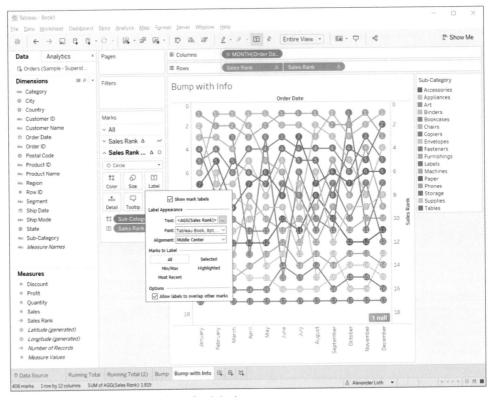

Figure 5.13 Formatting options for labels.

WINDOW_AVG is the operator for the moving average. It uses the value defined by the Time Period parameter as input for the window size.

Now, place the new Moving Average field on Rows, next to the Sales measure. With the dual-axis feature, you will once again place the two side-by-side charts on top of each other. Go into the context menu of the Moving Average field you just placed onto the view, and click Dual Axis. As before, ensure that the resulting two axes are synchronized by right-clicking the axis on the right and selecting Synchronize Axis.

The result is a line chart like the one in Figure 5.17, showing both the original time series (orange line) and its rolling average (blue line).

Try adjusting the parameter using the slider on the right side of the view. With this slider, you can adjust how smoothly you would like the blue line to trace out the long-term trend of the fluctuating line.

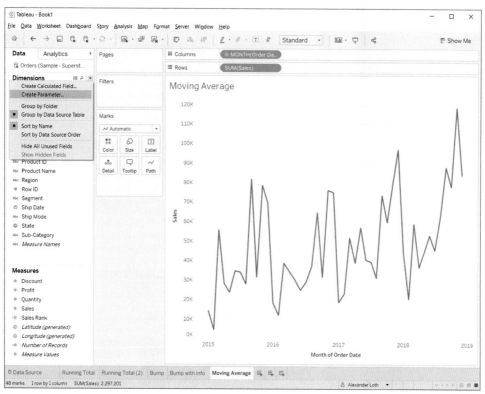

Figure 5.14 Line chart showing sales revenue over time, and the Data pane's context menu.

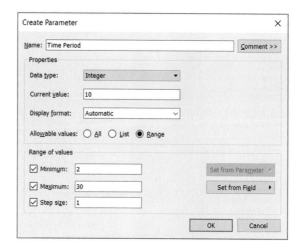

Figure 5.15 Settings for the Time Period parameter.

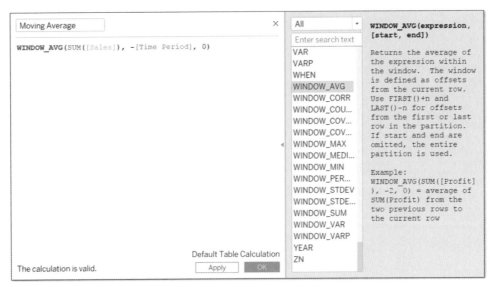

Figure 5.16 The formula for the moving average.

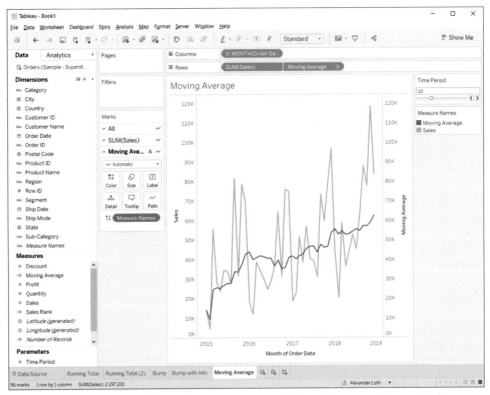

Figure 5.17 Line chart with moving average and dynamic parameter control.

LEVEL OF DETAIL EXPRESSIONS

With Level of Detail Expressions (often abbreviated LOD), you can manually specify the level of detail at which the aggregation of a calculated field happens, as opposed to having it evaluated at the level defined by the dimensions added to the view.

LOD Calculations share some similarities with Table Calculations, and some problems can be tackled equally well with either of them. But there are also significant differences and many use cases for which only one of the two methods is appropriate. One such difference is that LOD Calculations are calculated directly in the data source, meaning only the aggregated data needs to be transferred to Tableau. Assuming that the database has sufficient computing power, this can result in significant performance improvement.

The remainder of this chapter will look at the syntax, the three LOD keywords, and three interesting use cases of these types of calculations.

Keywords and Syntax

LOD Calculations are entered into calculated fields using the following syntax:

```
{ <LOD keyword> <Dimension(s)> : <Aggregate Calculation> }
```

The braces tell Tableau that you are using an LOD Expression. The last argument, `<Aggregate Calculation>`, is just a standard calculation with an aggregate function, as you have previously seen in many places in this book. The difference here is that with various keywords (`<LOD keyword>`) and by referring to specific dimensions in the data (`<Dimension(s)>`), you can specify the level of detail of the calculation. The keywords that can be used are as follows:

FIXED   The FIXED keyword is used to manually specify the dimensions that should define the level of detail, regardless of which dimensions are used in the chart.

A calculation with FIXED will also ignore dimensions and measures added to the Filter card. That is, the unfiltered data is used. LOD Calculations with FIXED can only be filtered by context filters, data source filters, and extract filters.

The following example calculates the sum of sales revenue for each segment. This could be added to a chart tooltip showing sales by transaction: when the user hovered over a mark, it would provide additional information about how much all customers spend in total in the same segment as the transaction in question:

```
{ FIXED [Segment] : SUM([Sales]) }
```

INCLUDE   The INCLUDE keyword is used to manually include another dimension (or several dimensions) in addition to those already used in the view.

Thus, the calculation's level of detail will be finer (in granularity) than that of the view. This is often used to explicitly specify the order of operations in a more complicated calculation: for example, to define the subunits across which to calculate a mean. We will look at this in more detail in the "Regional Averages" section.

Example:

```
{ INCLUDE [Customer Name] : SUM([Sales]) }
```

EXCLUDE   The EXCLUDE keyword is used to manually exclude another dimension (or several dimensions) from those already used in the view.

Thus, the calculation's level of detail will be coarser (in granularity) than that of the view.

Example:

```
{ EXCLUDE [Category] : SUM([Sales]) }
```

Cohort Analysis

What contribution do long-term customers make to sales? This is the type of question that can be answered in a cohort analysis. You want to group customers by the year of their first purchase and compare how much they spend. The simple calculation MIN([Order Date]) will give the first purchase, but you need to specify that you want this to always be the first order date for *each customer*. But this needs to be independent of the dimensions used in the view, because, in the end, you don't want to include the customer dimension in the view. On the contrary, you want an aggregate result across all customers within a cohort.

This is where an LOD Calculation can help. Create a new calculated field, call it First Purchase, and enter the following formula (see also Figure 5.18):

```
{ FIXED [Customer ID] : MIN([Order Date]) }
```

Before using this calculation, let's create a standard bar chart by putting the Sales measure on Rows and the Order Date dimension (as discrete years) on Columns. In the Marks card, change the mark type from Automatic to Bar.

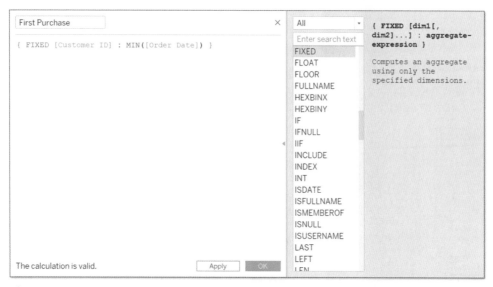

Figure 5.18 Calculated field to find the date of each customer's first purchase.

Now, add the newly created dimension First Purchase to Color. This breaks up the bars by cohorts as defined by the LOD formula; the result is the cohort analysis shown in Figure 5.19. You can see that customer loyalty pays off: a large fraction of revenue is from customers from the 2015 cohort.

Regional Averages

As you have seen, it is relatively easy to get Tableau to display the average sales revenue per region. All you have to do is add Region and Sales to the view and change the type of aggregation for Sales from sum to average. However, it is worth noting what you are averaging across. In this simple case, it's the sales transactions that happened in each region. After all, each line of the Superstore data set is a record of a single transaction. In other words, you get the average sales value of a transaction and how that differs by region.

Another average that could be interesting to look at is the average sales value per *customer* and how that differs by region. How do you calculate this in Tableau?

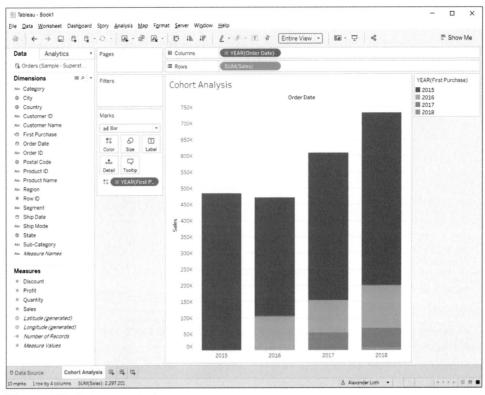

Figure 5.19 Cohort analysis.

You first need to know the sum of sales for each customer, before you can take the average of that. An LOD Expression can be used here. Create a new calculated field, call it `Sales per Customer`, and enter the following formula (see also Figure 5.20):

```
{ INCLUDE [Customer Name] : SUM([Sales]) }
```

By using the `SUM` operator in conjunction with the LOD Expression, you get the sum of sales for each customer. The `Customer Name` dimension is explicitly included because you would not want to add it to the view of the visualization; you want a chart showing the average across many different customers.

To create the previously mentioned chart, put the new field `Sales per Customer` onto Columns, and change the type of aggregation to Average (AVG). Then pull `Region` onto Rows in order to break up the result by region.

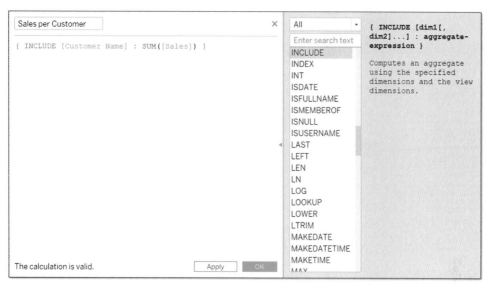

Figure 5.20 Calculated field yielding the total sales per customer.

It can be instructive to compare the result to the simple average of sales (across the transactions). To do so, add Sales to Columns, next to Sales per Customer. As you can see in Figure 5.21, average sales across transactions is similar in all four regions, whereas the average sales per customer in the regions East and West perform much better than those in Central and South.

Higher-Level Regions

In the previous example, you used INCLUDE to go one level deeper than the level of detail of the view, but often you want to do the opposite and include a calculation at a reduced level of detail in the chart. This serves to provide more context in which to evaluate the result of a single mark. To illustrate this, let's build a bar chart showing sales across both regions and subcategories. But let's add sales per subcategory at the national level as well (independent of region), so you can see how the regional performance varies from the overall performance.

To do this, create a calculated field with the name Sales across Regions, using the following formula (see also Figure 5.22):

```
{ EXCLUDE [Region] : SUM([Sales]) }
```

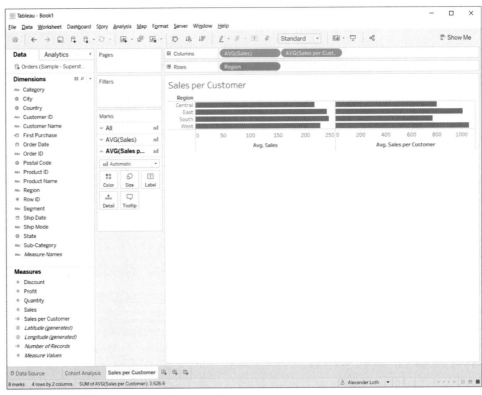

Figure 5.21 Different ways of calculating averages.

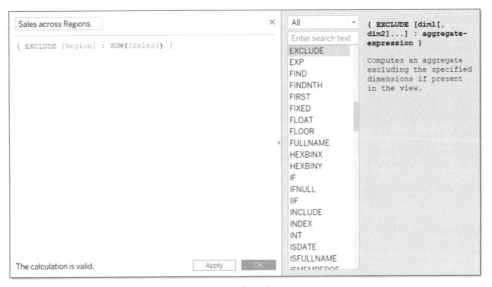

Figure 5.22 Sum of sales, independent of region.

In this field, Sales is aggregated across regions, even when the Region dimension is included in the view.

To build a bar chart, start by adding the Sales measure and the Region dimension to the Columns shelf. Then add the Sub-Category dimension to Rows. The result is a bar chart showing sales for each region and product.

Finally, add the Sales across Regions calculated field to Color. You may also want to click the Sort button on the toolbar to get the effect shown in Figure 5.23.

By adding the color gradient that shows sales by product across all regions, you can also see the overall pattern independent of region as context (in conjunction with the bars' sorting, which is also at the national level). You can identify, for example, that sales of chairs in South are relatively poor, although chairs are selling quite well across all four regions, as shown by the darker shaded bars.

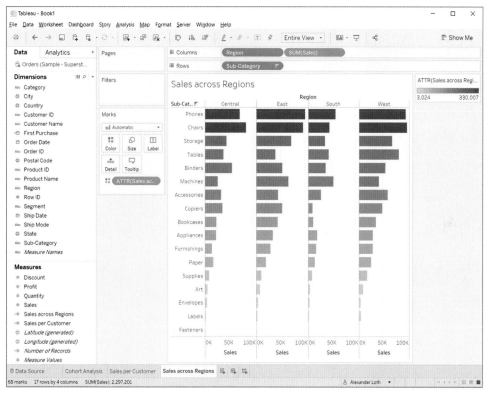

Figure 5.23 Bar chart showing how sales per subcategory at the regional level differ from those at the national level.

Chapter 6

Maps

From subway networks to weather forecasts to tourist guides, we are used to seeing maps conveying geographic information. When you want to display geographic data, you can utilize this familiarity to draw the end user into your data visualization. Furthermore, maps also help you see regional patterns that might be difficult to spot in a table.

Three basic map types in Tableau can be used to display geographic data in map form: symbol maps, filled maps, and density maps. With symbol maps, specific geographic locations are marked with circles, squares, or custom shapes. The form, size, or color of these marks can vary according to a measure or dimension.

With filled maps, also called choropleth maps, geographic areas are shaded according to a measure or dimension.

With density maps, also called heatmaps, areas of relative concentration are colored intensely, while those with sparse occurrences of the dimension in question are colored lightly. They are a good alternative to symbol maps when high concentrations of marks make it impossible to gauge the spatial distribution of individual marks.

Some of these map types can also be combined with each other, and sometimes it can make sense to add secondary information via a pop-up chart in the tooltips (a feature called *Viz in tooltip*).

Many commonly used geographic entities such as country, state, or city names are recognized by Tableau automatically. But you can also import spatial data to visualize more specialized geographic entities such as railway lines, cable networks, and custom sales territories.

By the end of this chapter, you will be able to:

◆ Create and combine symbol maps, filled maps, and density maps.

◆ Add visualizations to tooltips.

◆ Format your maps, work with different map services, and work with spatial files in Tableau.

SYMBOL MAPS

If Tableau recognizes that your data contains geographic dimensions (as indicated by the globe symbol next to the field name), it takes less than five seconds to create a map. Simply double-click the geographic dimension(s) you want to use, and then double-click one or more measures that you want to see on the map.

You can try this with the Superstore sample dataset by double-clicking first the three geographic dimensions Country, State, and City, and then the measure Sales. The geographic dimensions give you a symbol map showing the cities contained in the dataset, while Sales is automatically added to Size on the Marks card—meaning the size of the circles now reflects the sum of sales revenue coming from the different cities.

Double-clicking yet another measure such as Profit adds this measure to Color, and the circles are now shaded according to the sum of profits in the different cities. See Figure 6.1.

TIP Use the mouse wheel to quickly zoom in and out of a map. Moving the mouse while holding down the Shift key will pan the map.

TIP In the case of the Superstore dataset, the dimension City also requires you to add State and Country in order for Tableau to know exactly where to place the different cities in the dataset. If you create a geographic hierarchy by dragging City and State onto Country, you can subsequently add City more quickly by just double-clicking that dimension.

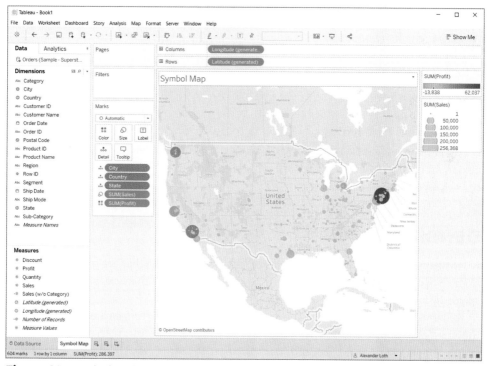

Figure 6.1 Symbol map with differently sized circles, based on the revenue in the different cities.

NOTE When all sub-entities are within a single geographic entity—e.g. a list of states within the United States—your dataset may not contain an extra column with the name of the top-level entity—i.e. a country column with "US" in all rows. So when you add the state field to the view, depending on the locale set in Tableau, it may not automatically recognize that the states are states within the United States. It will subsequently show an error message in the bottom-right corner of the map saying that not all states were recognized. You can remedy this by clicking the notification icon and manually setting the country to the United States.

FILLED MAPS

Filled maps that shade geographic areas in different colors can be created just as quickly as symbol maps.

First double-click a geographic dimension containing information about geographic areas, such as State. Note that to show all states, you also may need to add the Country dimension to the view, depending on the locale set in Tableau. The dimension City that you used for the symbol map would not work here, as there are no area outlines for cities saved in Tableau. Cities can only be shown as points on maps.

Again, add a measure such as Sales, and then open the Show Me menu. Click the button for filled maps (next to symbol maps, which should be highlighted in this case). See Figure 6.2.

TIP As you will have noticed, in Tableau, there's more than one way to accomplish tasks. Instead of using Show Me to get to a filled map, you could also switch the mark type from Automatic to Map in the drop-down menu of the Marks card (see Figure 6.3).

DENSITY MAPS

A density map, or heatmap, groups occurrences of a dimension that are geographically close to each other and colors the area in a more intense tone than areas with more sparse distributions.

To demonstrate this, return to the symbol map of US cities from earlier, but remove the Sales and Profit measures from the view. (If you prefer to start with a blank canvas, simply double-click City, State, and Country to get the same result.) You get a simple

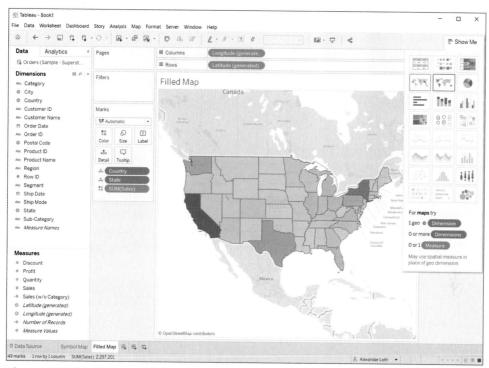

Figure 6.2 Filled map with states shaded according to the sum of sales.

Figure 6.3 Creating a filled map by selecting the appropriate mark type in the Marks card.

dot map that shows in which cities you have customers. Some regions, such as the San Francisco Bay Area, for example, have high concentrations of dots. Because of the overlapping dots, it is difficult to spot any spatial patterns. This issue is sometimes referred to as *over-plotting*.

Change the mark type in the Marks card to Density, and you can see that the concentration is actually much higher in Southern California compared to further north in the Bay Area. See Figure 6.4.

MAP LAYERS

Tableau maps consist of two components: background maps and the marks shown on top. Tableau's default background map comes in three styles: Light, Normal, and Dark.

These can be selected by choosing Maps and then Map Layers in the main menu. In addition to the style, many other components of the background map can be configured in the Map Layers pane, as shown in Figure 6.5.

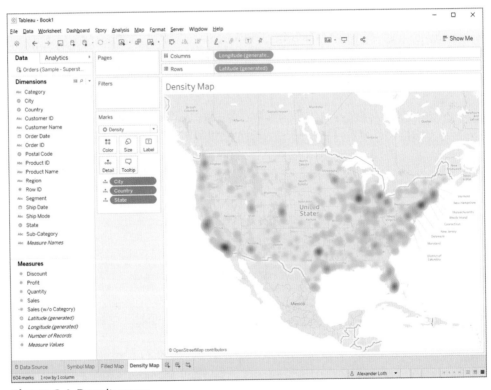

Figure 6.4 Density map.

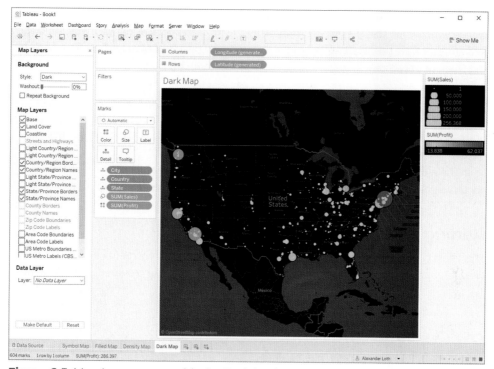

Figure 6.5 Map Layers pane with the Dark background map style selected.

These include borders, coastlines, and country names. The Data Layer section offers the possibility to add certain socio-economic statistics as shaded areas to the background map. These are only available for the territory of the United States.

TIP Some of the map-layer options are greyed out at certain zoom levels. To toggle these options on or off, zoom in on the map first by clicking the plus button in the top-left corner of the map or by using the mouse scroll wheel.

MAPS WITH PIE CHARTS

Since maps use the horizontal and vertical position to encode geographic locations, you have fewer options to encode data values than with other chart types. However, there are ways to add more information to maps. One popular option is the pie chart map. This is a variant of the symbol map that allows you to show proportions of a nongeographic dimension.

These kinds of maps can quickly become overloaded with marks. If that happens, it can be worthwhile to try a filter to show only the most important marks. If you need to add another field to the view, you can also combine a pie chart map with a filled map via the Dual Axis feature.

Creating a Pie Chart Map

Start by creating a simple symbol map: double-click City, State, and Country. Then double-click the Sales measure to add it to Size.

In the mark type menu on the Marks card, change the type to Pie. Finally, move Category to Color. This breaks the pies into different-sized wedges—see Figure 6.6.

Adding a Filter

This chart type could work well at the state level. (Give it a try by removing City from the view.) But I think you will agree that the city-level map is a little crowded. It might make

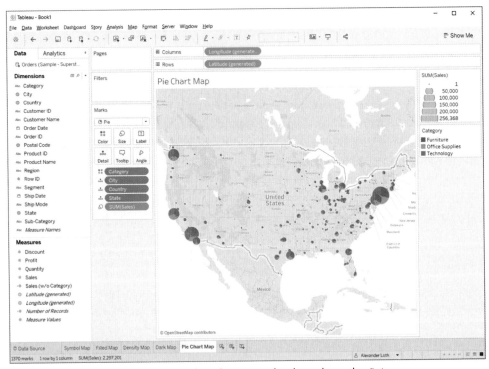

Figure 6.6 Map with pie charts showing Sales broken down by Category.

sense to focus only on the most important cities, as measured by total sales revenue. However, if you were to simply add Sales to the Filters card, you would filter the individual categories.

To avoid filtering out individual pie segments, you need to use an LOD Expression. Create a new calculated field, call it Sales (w/o Category), and enter the following formula:

```
{ EXCLUDE [Category] : SUM([Sales]) }
```

Then add the new field to the Filters card and select Attribute in the Filter Field dialog box. Right-click the new filter to open its context menu, and select Show Filter. As shown in Figure 6.7, the map can now be filtered by sales revenue using the slider control.

Dual Axis Map

As previously mentioned, one way to bring in another measure is to add a filled map behind the pie charts. You can add Profit, for example, via a dual-axis chart.

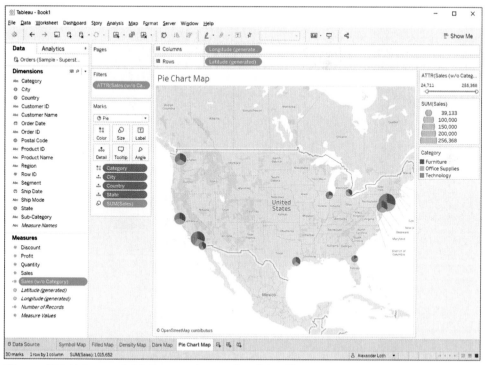

Figure 6.7 Using an LOD Expression and a slider filter to declutter the map.

To do so, drag another instance of the field Latitude (Generated) from the Data pane to the Rows shelf. In the context menu of one of the two Latitude (Generated) fields, select Dual Axis.

As shown in Figure 6.8, you now have two overlaid maps with two separate Marks cards.

TIP In a dual axis chart, you can change which of the two charts is on top and which is underneath by switching the position of the two measures used to construct the chart (in this case, the Latitude (Generated) measure on the Rows shelf). Typically, you will want the marks of the symbol map to lie on top of those of the filled map. Therefore, the field for the symbol map should be on the right.

VIZ IN TOOLTIP

The dual-axis map from the previous section tried to cram a lot of information into one chart. In this section, let's try a more gentle way of introducing more information to a

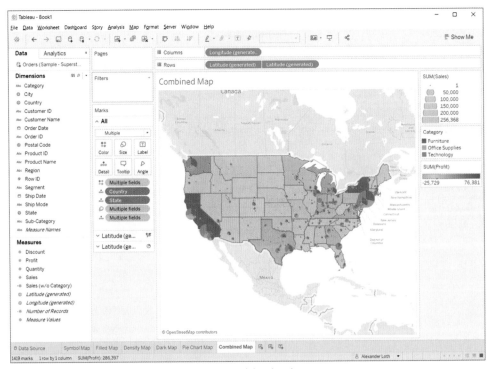

Figure 6.8 A dual-axis chart: filled map with pie charts.

map. You will add a second chart to the tooltips that will be seen when you hover over individual marks on the map.

This feature, called Viz in Tooltip, is not restricted to maps, but it is particularly useful with maps. It allows you to hold back information that is perhaps only relevant at a second glance. A good example would be a symbol map showing overall sales revenue and a tooltip showing how it breaks down by product categories and how it has changed over time.

Step 1: Create the Second Chart

Let's create this visualization using the Superstore data set. Start by creating the chart that will be shown in the tooltip. In this case, you want it to be a line chart.

Open a new worksheet, call it Over Time, and then add the following fields to the view: Sales to Rows, Order Date to Columns, and Category to Color. The result should look like Figure 6.9.

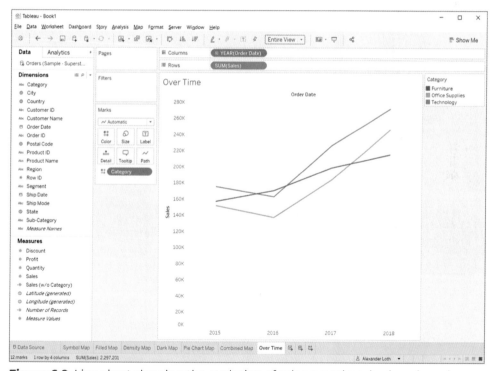

Figure 6.9 Line chart showing the evolution of sales over time, broken down by product category.

Step 2: Embedding the Chart in Tooltips

Create the main chart, a symbol map, as introduced at the beginning of this chapter. In the Marks card, click Tooltip.

The subsequent dialog box, Edit Tooltip, lets you modify the content shown in the tooltip. Since you are adding an entire chart, it is probably best to remove what appears in the text field automatically. Then choose Insert, Sheets, and look for the name of the line chart you just created (Over Time), as shown in Figure 6.10.

After you have successfully edited the tooltip, you can hover over different cities on the symbol map. The tooltip will include the relevant line chart for the city, as shown in Figure 6.11.

TIP It is possible to include several charts and text fields in a tooltip. However, it is recommended that you keep them to a reasonable size so they don't block the entire chart underneath. If you find yourself including a lot of information in a tooltip, you may want to consider creating a dashboard instead, as described in Chapter 8.

Figure 6.10 Embedding the Over Time chart via the Edit Tooltip dialog.

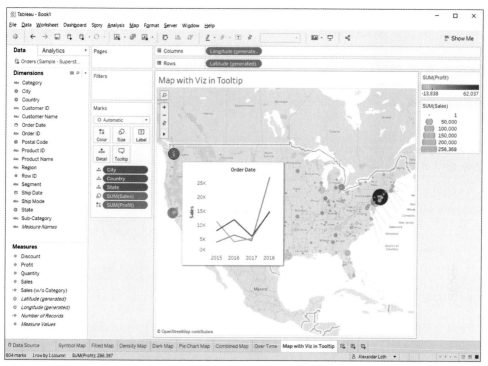

Figure 6.11 Tooltip with embedded line chart that appears when hovering over marks.

REFLECTION: THE ANATOMY OF A TABLEAU MAP

When you create a map by adding a geographic field (a dimension marked with the globe symbol) to the view, the following processes happen in the background:

- Tableau looks up the longitude and latitude of the geographic entries and adds the information to two new fields. These fields are added to the Rows and Column shelves and provide the coordinates for the chart's marks.

- In the case of filled maps, Tableau looks up the shapes of the different geographic areas and styles the marks accordingly.

- Tableau also adds a background map to provide more context for the individual marks. By default, this map is provided by OpenStreetMap.

You can manually intervene in all three of these processing steps, to fine-tune your chart or to create even more advanced maps.

If a dimension is not recognized as a geographic field, you can provide the coordinates manually by adding latitude and longitude as separate fields. For example, you may have a list of coordinates with your company's production facilities. Shapes that are unknown to Tableau (as well as coordinates) can also be added via *spatial files*. Finally, there are several (more colorful!) alternatives to the (grey) OpenStreetMap background maps. The following sections will describe these features in more detail.

TIP It is possible to merge existing shapes with new geographic entities. One way is to group them using the lasso tool found in the menu in the top-left corner of the map. Then remove the original geographic dimension and watch how the areas are combined into new, larger entities. With this trick you can, for example, map the sales revenue coming from different sales territories, such as APAC, EMEA, and North America, as opposed to showing it for individual countries.

ALTERNATIVE MAP SERVICES

The Map menu gives you a choice of what type of background map to use for your visualization:

Tableau   When you are connected to the internet, you can use the default maps, which are provided by the free Wiki project OpenStreetMap (OSM). The maps from OSM are very detailed and always up to date; many volunteers worldwide contribute to the open geodatabase on which these are based.

Offline Maps   Should you find yourself without an internet connection, you can also switch to the offline maps that are included with your installation of Tableau Desktop. To do so, from the Map menu, choose Background Maps, and select Offline. Note, however, that these maps are not as detailed as the online maps.

Map Services   If you are not happy with these out-of-the box maps, you can replace them with custom maps from other online map services. In the Map menu, select Background Maps and then Map Services. You can now connect to any Web Map Service (WMS) server you have access to. This menu also allows you to connect to the Mapbox map service, which is relatively well integrated into Tableau—see the "Mapbox Maps" section for more details.

Background Images   You can also use your own images, such as a building floorplan, as background maps, if your spatial data is too detailed to be plotted on a standard map. To do so, choose Background Images from the Map menu.

MAPBOX MAPS

Mapbox is a service for creating customized online maps. Users who do not exceed a certain limit in terms of page views can work with a free account. The current limit is 50,000 views per month, which should be sufficient for many use cases.

The Mapbox Studio tool lets you design your own maps, but you can also work in Tableau with the ready-made templates provided by Mapbox, which we will look at now.

Mapbox Account and Token

To use these templates, you need to sign up for a free account at www.mapbox.com. On the same website, navigate to Access Tokens. Copy the default public token (the key starting with pk) to the clipboard. If none is shown, click Create A Token (see Figure 6.12).

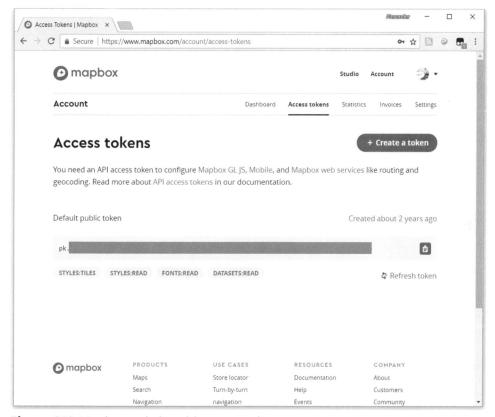

Figure 6.12 Mapbox website with access token.

Mapbox in Tableau

As mentioned previously, the connection to Mapbox is set up by selecting Map, Background Maps, Map Services, as shown in Figure 6.13.

In the Map Services dialog box, click Add and then Mapbox Maps, as shown in Figure 6.14.

You see the Add Mapbox Map window, which has two tabs:

- **Mapbox GL:** Choose this to embed custom maps created in Mapbox Studio.
- **Classic:** Choose this to use predefined templates in Mapbox Styles.

Let's try this with the popular satellite-image background map. Select Classic, and enter a Style Name of your choosing, e.g. Satellite. Next, paste the Mapbox token from the clipboard into the API Access Token field. In the Mapbox Preset Style field, select Satellite, and click OK (see Figure 6.15).

Using the Background Map

Mapbox maps are used just like the standard background maps in Tableau. Simply double-click your geographic dimensions to show them on the map. For example, try adding Country, State, and City.

You should see a map similar to the one in Figure 6.16. Try adjusting the size and color (including the borders and halos) of the marks to get a good contrast to the attractive but admittedly busy-looking background photo. You can also change the mark type to Shape and experiment with different forms of marks.

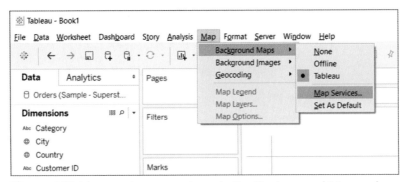

Figure 6.13 Map services are set up via the Background Maps submenu.

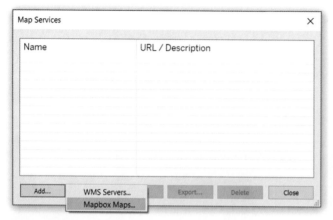

Figure 6.14 Map Services dialog with the Add button clicked.

SPATIAL DATA

Spatial data, including both geographic coordinates and areas, is often stored in certain file formats. Tableau supports the following spatial file formats:

- KML files (*.kml), an XML-based standard created by the Open Geospacial Consortium and popularized by the Google Earth tool.

Figure 6.15 Selecting a Mapbox preset style.

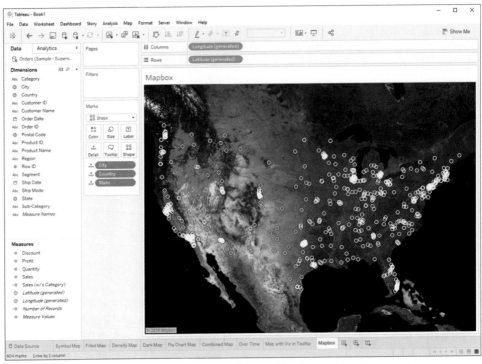

Figure 6.16 Cities in the dataset on top of a satellite-image background map.

- ESRI Shapefiles (*.shp), which is the leading file format in the world of GIS mapping.
- MapInfo TAB format (*.tab).
- MapInfo Interchange Format (*.mif).
- GeoJSON files (*geojson), an open standard based on the JSON format. (Standard JSON files can also be opened in Tableau.)

With these file types, you can map geographic data that goes beyond the basic entities such as countries, states, and cities that are stored in Tableau's internal database. Next, we will look at a real-world example.

Undersea Communication Cables

For this example, we won't use the Superstore dataset used for most of the examples in this book so far. Instead, you will download a spatial file from the website https://cablemap.info/_default.aspx. It contains information about the world's major undersea cables, which connect the telecommunication networks of the different continents. What you want to do is map the routes of these cables and add some quantitative information such as capacity and distance.

NOTE Inspiration for this chart comes from a visualization by Ben Jones, formerly director for Tableau Public at Tableau, now founder at Data Literacy (https://public.tableau.com/en-us/s/blog/2017/08/blazing-trail-tableau-public-104).

Start by downloading the data by clicking Raw Data in the top-right corner of the website (see Figure 6.17) or by going directly to the following URL: http://www.cablemap.info/gregs_cable_map_v1.58.zip.

Unpack the Zip file in a folder on your hard drive. Then open a new instance of Tableau and, under Connect, click Spatial File, as shown in Figure 6.18.

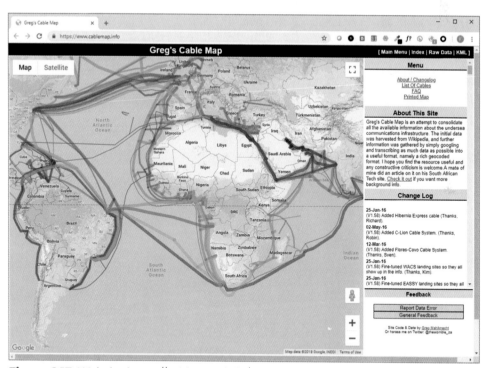

Figure 6.17 Website https://cablemap.info/_default.aspx.

In the Open dialog box, navigate to the folder with the data, and open the file Cables.shp, as shown in Figure 6.19.

On the Data Source page, where you now see a preview of the data in this Shapefile (see Figure 6.20). Notice that all spatial files contain a geofield (with a globe symbol) called Geometry. It stores the geographic locations and shapes that you want to show on the map. The other fields may be dimensions that break the data into different entities (e.g. Name in this case) or measures with additional quantitative information about the various geographic entities (e.g. Capacity G and Distance K). Often, however, the spatial file will only contain the geographic information and perhaps a name field, and you will have to join the dataset with other datasets to enrich it with interesting quantitative information.

Figure 6.18 Connecting to spatial files.

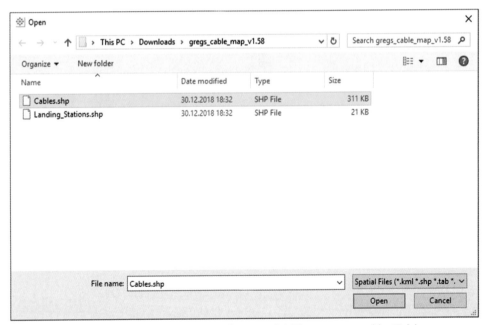

Figure 6.19 The Open dialog box showing spatial files supported by Tableau.

NOTE The Shapefile file format is the de facto standard in the world of Geographic Information System (GIS). As such, the majority of open data map data is available as Shapefiles. Shapefiles can be created and edited with the open source tool QGIS (www.qgis.org).

Go to Sheet 1. There, double-click the field Geometry. Doing so creates a map showing the entire network of undersea cables. When you hover over it with the mouse, you will notice that it is essentially one large mark. To break it into smaller units, you need to add the dimension Name, by double-clicking it or by dragging it onto Detail on the Marks card. Now you see one mark for each named segment of the network.

Next, add your measures. Place the field Distance K on Color, to visually highlight the longer segments that now are colored a darker shade of blue.

To make the chart look like the one in Figure 6.21, also open the context menu of the Name field on the Marks card, and click Sort. In the dialog box, select Sort By: Field, Sort

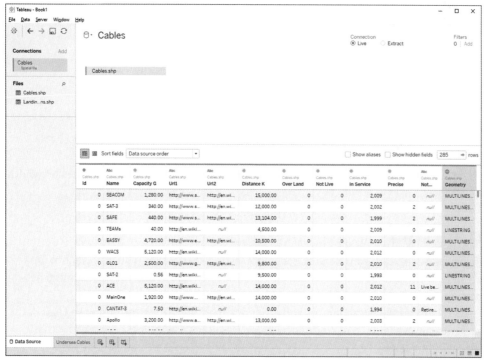

Figure 6.20 Data model and preview of the Shapefile.

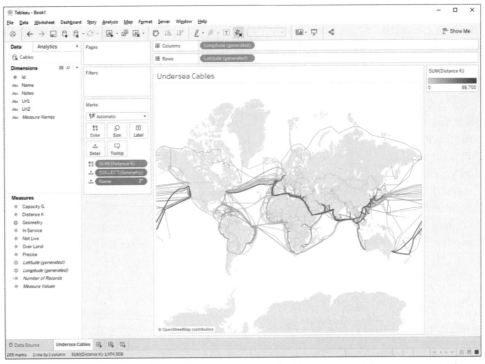

Figure 6.21 World map with undersea communication cables. Marks are sorted and shaded according to the length of the different network segments.

Order: Descending, and Field Name: Distance K. This ensures that the marks of the shorter segments are not overlapping those of the longer segments.

If you want to, you can also try adding Capacity G to Size, which determines the width of the lines.

Open Data

If you are keen to try your hand at other interesting spatial files, you may want to look at some of the prominent open data portals. These of course are not restricted to geographic data.

Many United Nations agencies and other international organizations make their datasets publicly available. The World Bank Open Data portal is the best example: https://data.worldbank.org.

In the United States, over 300,000 datasets are available for download from https://www.data.gov. In the UK, a similar portal is https://data.gov.uk.

Cities and local communities also have interesting datasets, such as the London Datastore provided by the Mayor of London (https://data.london.gov.uk/dataset).

The EU makes geographic data available via the INSPIRE portal (http://inspire-geoportal.ec.europa.eu/). Macroeconomic data can be found in the Statistical Data Warehouse of the European Central Bank (http://sdw.ecb.europa.eu) (see Figure 6.22); and environmental data, including many spatial files, can be found on the website of the European Environment Agency (https://www.eea.europa.eu/data-and-maps).

NOTE INSPIRE (INfrastructure for SPatial InfoRmation in Europe) is an initiative to establish a common geodata infrastructure in Europe. For more information, see https://en.wikipedia.org/wiki/Infrastructure_for_Spatial_Information_in_the_European_Community.

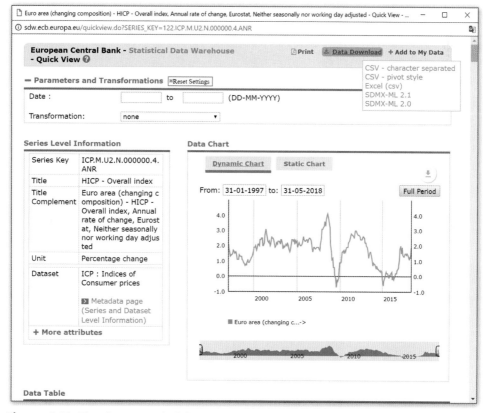

Figure 6.22 The data portal of the European Central Bank.

These are just a couple examples out of many, but they should offer a good starting point into the world of spatial data, in particular, and open data more generally.

TIP Data portals often give you a choice of which format you want to use. Spatial data should come in one of the formats listed at the beginning of this chapter. For other types of data, JSON, Excel, and CSV are among the commonly used formats in the open data world that can also be read by Tableau. If you have a choice, select Excel files over CSV files, because the latter sometimes require you to specify exactly what characters are used as column and decimal separators. Avoid data that has been preaggregated or pivoted; Tableau works best with unaggregated data.

Chapter 7

Advanced Analytics: Trends, Forecasts, Clusters, and other Statistical Tools

In Tableau Desktop, you can run statistical analyses with only a few clicks. Tableau's advanced analytics tools include distribution bands, trend lines, forecasts, and clustering. With these tools, you can tackle analytical questions that cannot be answered with simple descriptive visualizations. But they don't return simple summary tables as results; instead, as Tableau is primarily a visual analytics tool, the output is added to the charts you create.

In addition to the built-in analytics tools, it is possible to integrate Tableau with different programming languages for more sophisticated, customized analytics projects. This integration of Python, R, and MATLAB will be covered in the second half of this chapter.

By the end of this chapter, you will be able to:

- Answer complex statistical questions using the Tableau Analytics pane.
- Show trends, clusters, and forecasts based on your data.
- Use the integration of the programming languages Python, R, and MATLAB for more advanced analyses.

OVERVIEW OF THE TABLEAU ANALYTICS PANE

Tableau's advanced analytics tools can be found in the Analytics pane, which sits behind the Data pane on the left side of the screen. The tools are grouped as follows:

Summarize:

- **Constant Line:** Adds a line to the chart, intersecting the axis at a fixed value of your choosing—see the "Constant, Average, and Reference Lines" section.
- **Average Line:** Adds one or several average lines to your view, based on the arithmetic mean of the chart's data—see the "Constant, Average, and Reference Lines" section.
- **Median with Quartiles:** Adds one or more sets of median lines with distribution bands to your view.
- **Box Plot:** Adds one or more box plots to your view.
- **Totals:** Adds subtotals, column grand totals, or row grand totals to your view.

Model:

- **Average with 95% CI:** Adds one or more sets of average lines with distribution bands to your view. The bands show the 95% confidence interval around the data's mean.
- **Median with 95% CI:** Adds one or more sets of median lines with distribution bands to your view. The bands show the 95% confidence interval around the data's median.
- **Trend Line:** Adds one or more trend lines to your view—see the "Trend Lines" section.

- **Forecast:** Adds a forecast to your view—see the "Forecasts" section.
- **Cluster:** Runs a clustering algorithm—see the "Cluster Analysis" section.

Custom:
- **Reference Line:** Adds one or more lines reflecting the value of additional measures, calculations, or parameters.
- **Reference Band:** Adds one or more bands reflecting the values of additional measures, calculations, or parameters.
- **Distribution Band:** Adds a shaded band showing the distribution of the chart's data along an axis, as measured by percentages, percentiles, quantiles, or the standard deviation.
- **Box Plot:** Adds one or more customizable box plots to your view.

These tools are applied to a chart simply by dragging and dropping them onto the canvas. Depending on what measures and dimensions you use, some items may be greyed out. But in all cases, you will need at least one measure on your view.

In this chapter we will focus on the slightly more complicated tools, and on those that are most commonly used in a business context.

CONSTANT, AVERAGE, AND REFERENCE LINES

To show a certain threshold value, a benchmark, or a ceiling in your visualization, you drag the item Constant Line onto the view. You will be able to choose the value of the constant, as shown in Figure 7.1.

Average Line, on the other hand, will add a line determined by the arithmetic mean of all the marks in the chosen partition (for the whole table, for each individual pane, or for each cell, as defined by the dimensions in the view). And the Reference Line tool will let you add a line whose position is determined by another measure, a calculated field, or a parameter.

TIP To edit an existing line, reference band, distribution band, or box plot, simply click the object in the view and select Edit.

TREND LINES

Line charts can sometimes be difficult to interpret when the data is very granular. Trend lines help you to see the pattern in your data, by tracing out the fundamental evolution of the measure in question.

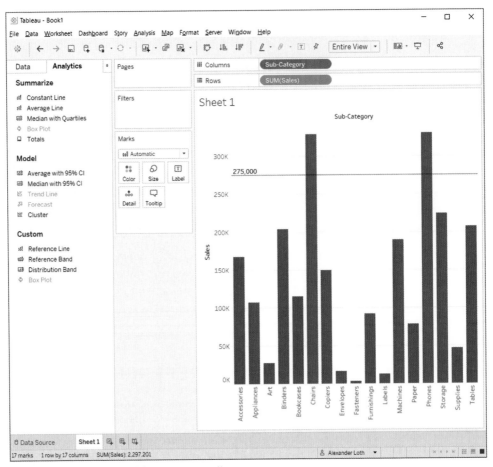

Figure 7.1 Bar chart with a constant line.

The following trend line models are available:

- Linear
- Logarithmic
- Exponential
- Polynomial
- Power

Adding Trend Lines

To add a trend line, drag the Trend Line item from the Analytics pane to your view. While you are moving the mouse, Tableau will show a selection of the available types of regression models (see Figure 7.2).

Choose the model type that is most appropriate for your use case by dropping the Trend Line on the respective field. Models that are not compatible with your data are greyed out and can't be selected.

The line chart in Figure 7.3 shows a polynomial trend line that captures the underlying trend of the volatile monthly revenue figures.

Figure 7.2 Selection fields with different types of trend line models.

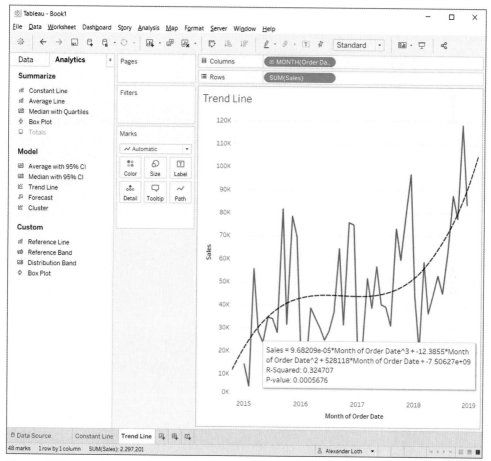

Figure 7.3 Line chart with an added trend line and its tooltip.

As you can see, the volatility of the data makes it difficult to discern the overall trend. It is not a very tight fit, but the trend line helps you to see that, over the long run, revenues are trending up.

TIP When you hover over the trend line, a tooltip will pop up, providing you with the trend line's formula (the regression equation), the R^2 statistic (also called the *coefficient of determination*), as well as the p-value (the probability value, used for assessing the model's overall significance).

Trend Line Options

To configure your trend line, right-click the line, and select Edit Trend Lines. A dialog box with the options shown in Figure 7.4 opens.

Among other things, this lets you retrospectively change the model type and adjust the degree of polynomial trend lines.

If your view includes a dimension on Color, you can have a separate trend line for each group of marks of a certain color, by selecting Allow A Trend Line Per Color. Checking the Show Confidence Bands box will display the lower and upper bounds of the 95%-confidence interval around the estimated line. When using the trend line in scatter plots, you can have the line cut the vertical axis at the origin, by selecting the option Force Y-intercept To Zero. You can also choose whether to show tooltips and recalculated lines for selected data points.

Figure 7.4 Dialog box with trend line options.

Line and Trend Model Description

How accurate is your trend line? You can answer this question by right-clicking the line and selecting Describe Trend Line. Tableau will show you the regression equation and the p-value for its overall significance, as shown in Figure 7.5.

If you require further information about the estimated model, choose Describe Trend Model in the same context menu. The window shown in Figure 7.6 will give you a detailed overview of the model's statistics.

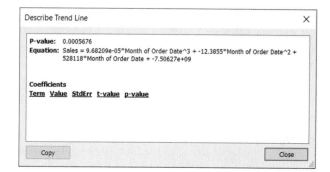

Figure 7.5 Description of a trend line.

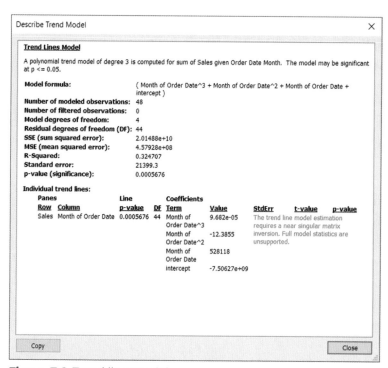

Figure 7.6 Trend line model.

The trend model description shows you the statistics of the model underlying your trend line. Even if you do not have a background in statistics, you may appreciate the importance of the p-value, which helps you assess the significance and hence the predictive value of the trend line. A commonly used level of significance is 0.05. If the p-value is larger than that, the trend line does not have much value for making inferences.

FORECASTS

Forecasting models extrapolate future values of a time series based on its historical values, allowing you to attempt to predict the evolution of a measure. Many different mathematical models can be used for such endeavors, each with its own advantages and drawbacks. Tableau's forecasting tool uses what is called *exponential smoothing*.

In such models, more recent data points are assigned greater weights than older observations. They work reasonably well to capture both long-term trends and any potential seasonality that may be present in the time series. The resulting forecast is shown directly in the chart.

Because we are talking about time-series data, ensure that your view contains a time or date field as well as a measure.

Adding a Forecast Line to the View

To illustrate the process, let's try to predict sales revenue for the next year using the Superstore dataset.

Create a line chart, with Sales on Rows and Order Date (as continuous months) on Columns. Then, drag the Forecast item from the Analytics pane to the canvas. Your chart will be expanded with the forecasted values, which are shown in a lighter color (see Figure 7.7).

Forecast Settings

As is so often the case in Tableau, when you add the forecast feature via drag-and-drop, a few things happen in the background. Tableau automatically sets the following:

- The forecast length
- The aggregation and range of the historical data going into the forecast model
- The model equation
- The prediction interval and its confidence level

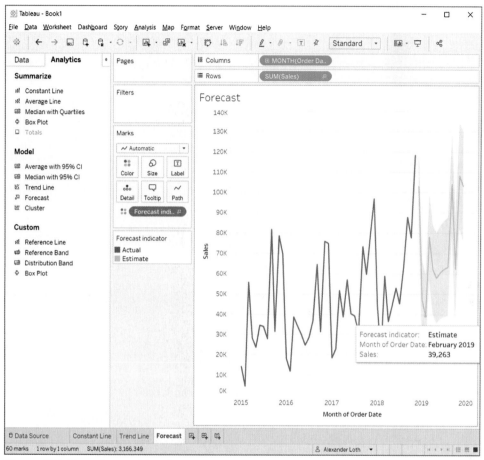

Figure 7.7 Line chart with a forecast.

If you would like to set these parameters manually instead, you can do so by right-clicking anywhere on your chart and selecting Forecast, Forecast Options in the context menu. The Forecast Options window will appear (see Figure 7.8).

As you can see, for this chart, Tableau suggests a forecast length of 13 months. This length was chosen based on the amount of historical data available, but you can change this value in accordance with your needs.

The Ignore Last field allows you to leave out data for incomplete months that might skew the results.

Missing values are automatically excluded from forecast models in Tableau. Depending on the situation, this may be the right thing to do. But there are cases where it can make sense to activate the option Fill In Missing Values With Zeroes.

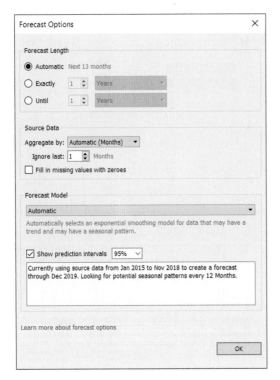

Figure 7.8 Forecast Options dialog box.

You can choose from among the following forecast models:

- Automatic
- Automatic Without Seasonality
- Custom

Depending on the quantity and level of detail of your data, these models yield different results. With Automatic, Tableau tries to model both a long-term trend and seasonal variation. With Automatic Without Seasonality, Tableau only models the trend. With Custom, you can specify manually what type of model to use for the trend and for the seasonality.

Model Description

Detailed information about the model used in the forecast can be obtained by right-clicking the chart and choosing Forecast, Describe Forecast. The Describe Forecast window will appear.

As shown in Figure 7.9, the Summary tab provides an assessment of the model's accuracy and the quality of the predicted values. The latter is returned as Good, Ok, or Poor.

The Models tab provides more details on the model type, quality metrics, and smoothing coefficients. See Figure 7.10.

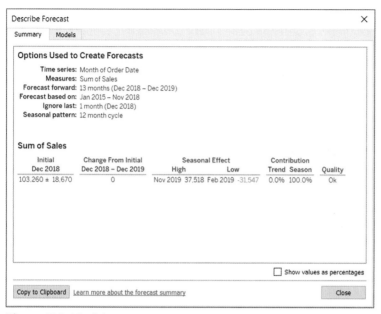

Figure 7.9 Model summary.

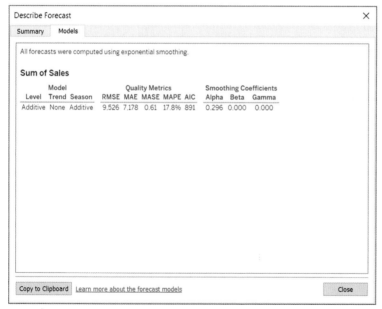

Figure 7.10 Model type, quality metrics, and smoothing coefficients.

The forecast models used by Tableau assign greater weight to more recent observations. The smoothing coefficients determine the extent to which this happens. A value close to 1 indicates that only recent values influence the forecast. A value of 0 means all historical data enters the equation equally (maximum smoothing). The alpha coefficient refers to the level forecast, the beta coefficient to the trend forecast, and the gamma coefficient to the forecast of the seasonality.

CLUSTER ANALYSIS

A *cluster* is a collection of data points with similar properties. Cluster analysis helps you find such groupings in your data. A classic use case comes from the field of marketing, where clustering is often used to define different customer segments.

The clustering tool in Tableau uses the widely used k-means algorithm, a type of vector quantization developed originally in the field of signal processing. Simply put, the method works by assigning *n* number of observations to *k* number of clusters, so that each observation is part of the cluster with the nearest cluster mean.

Clustering in Tableau

Scatter plots lend themselves to demonstrating the clustering method. Therefore, let's use this chart type to try the clustering tool in Tableau. Assume that you want to segment the customers in the Superstore sample dataset using two variables: profitability and sales volume. Start by creating the scatter plot: place Profit on Rows and Sales on Columns. Then add Customer ID to Detail on the Marks card, in order to get one mark per customer.

From the Analytics pane, drag the Cluster item onto the view. Tableau creates a new dimension called Clusters and places it on the Color field of the Marks card. In addition, a window opens that lets you make changes to the cluster analysis.

Tableau automatically suggests a number of distinct clusters. In this case, it divides the marks into two segments. But you can also constrain the number of clusters to a number of your choosing. Enter a number between 2 and 50 in the Number Of Clusters field. For example, try entering 4 in that field. The result should look like the chart in Figure 7.11.

You can also add more variables to the cluster model by dragging fields from the Data pane onto the list of Variables in the Clusters window.

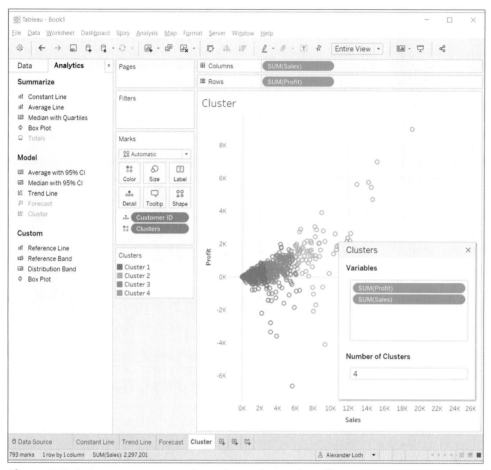

Figure 7.11 Customer segments based on sales and profits.

Saving and Working with Clustering Results

To save the results of a cluster analysis, you can drag the newly created Clusters field from the Marks card to the Data pane. Give the field a name or confirm the one suggested (in this case, Customer ID (clusters)). You can now find the field in the Dimensions section of the Data pane and use it like any other field.

You can, for example, use the field in the example to see how the different cluster segments are distributed across the regions in the data set. Open a new sheet in the same workbook. Then put Sales onto Rows and Region onto Columns. Also pull the newly created clusters field Customer ID (clusters) onto Columns, as shown in Figure 7.12.

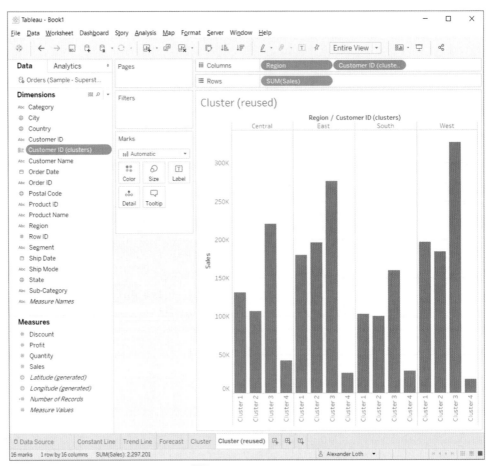

Figure 7.12 Working with the clusters field for Customer ID.

This is just a simple example of how you can continue to work with the results of a cluster analysis to ask further questions about your data.

PYTHON, R, AND MATLAB INTEGRATION

As you have seen, the Analytics pane offers quick access to a handful of useful analytics tools. However, if you require deeper statistical analysis of your data to complement Tableau's visual analytics approach, it is often necessary to use one of the popular data science tools: Python, R, or MATLAB. Beginning with the 2013 version, it has been possible to use Tableau together with the programming language R, meaning you can add calculated fields with R scripts to the view to visualize the results of calculations run in R. In subsequent years, Python and MATLAB integrations were added to provide similar functionality with these two tools. As you can imagine, this opens up a world of advanced statistical analyses that can be performed with your data.

Tableau supports the integration of these three services:

R   R is an open source programming language widely used in the scientific community because of its many packages for statistical analysis and the creation of statistical charts.

MATLAB   MATLAB is a software package with a mathematics-focused syntax. It is often used in signal processing, in testing and measurement processes, in financial modelling, and in the field of bioinformatics.

Python   Python is a popular general-purpose programming language used both in academia and in many business applications. Python includes a number of statistical and machine learning tools out of the box and, like R, can be extended by adding modules created by the Python community.

For the examples in this chapter, I will focus on Python and R, due to their popularity with data scientists. The MATLAB integration works much the same way, so I will only briefly touch on how to configure a connection to the MATLAB Production Server at the end of this chapter.

Getting Started with Python and TabPy

To use Python in Tableau, you need to install TabPy. TabPy includes the Python distribution called Anaconda, so a separate installation of Python is not strictly necessary.

To install TabPy, navigate to the following GitHub repository: https://github.com/tableau/TabPy. Click Clone Or Download in the top-right corner of the web page, as shown in Figure 7.13. Then select Download ZIP. Once the file is downloaded, extract its contents into a new folder (e.g. C:\Downloads\TabPy\).

Readers familiar with Git can also download TabPy directly using the following command (see also Figure 7.14):

```
git clone git://github.com/tableau/TabPy
```

Run the extracted installer (setup.bat on a Windows machine, setup.sh on a Mac). The script will download and install Python, TabPy, and all necessary components. Afterward, TabPy will start up automatically and begin to receive incoming signals via port 9004.

Figure 7.13 The GitHub repository for TabPy.

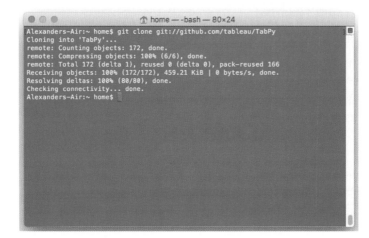

Figure 7.14 Downloading TabPy via the Git command line (here shown on a Mac).

Connecting Tableau with TabPy

In Tableau Desktop, open the Help menu, go to Settings And Performance, and then choose Manage External Service Connection. See Figure 7.15.

In the External Service Connection window, choose TabPy/External API. Fill in the Server and Port fields according to the TabPy installation. If TabPy runs on the same machine as Tableau Desktop, the server is `localhost`. Typically the port used by TabPy is 9004 (see Figure 7.16).

Finally, click the Test Connection button. Should the connection fail, Tableau will show an error message. In that case, click Show Details to see the log provided by the server.

TIP You can also have TabPy installed on another machine in order to use that machine's computing power for the calculations. If you do that, you only have to supply the host name of the computer on which TabPy runs when configuring the connection. Also, be sure the firewall doesn't block the port in question.

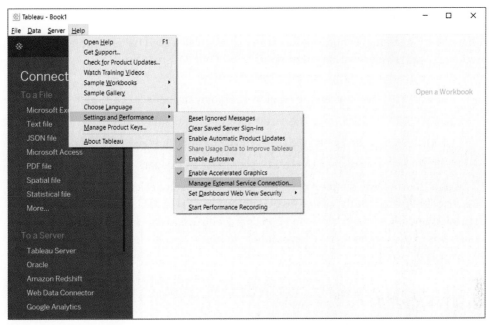

Figure 7.15 The Help menu and the Settings And Performance submenu.

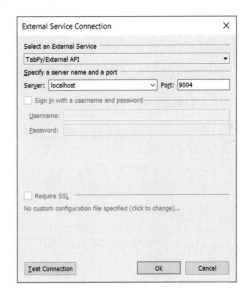

Figure 7.16 External Service Connection window to configure a local TabPy connection.

Python Scripts in Calculated Fields

Once the connection is set up, you can start creating calculated fields in Tableau with Python scripts for more advanced computations. Four different functions tell Tableau that you are providing a script for an external service:

- SCRIPT_STR is used when the result returned by the service is a string variable.
- SCRIPT_REAL is used when the result returned is a number.
- SCRIPT_BOOL is used when the expected result is of the True/False kind.
- SCRIPT_INT is used when the result returned is an integer.

Listing 7.1 provides a simple example: the formula used to calculate the correlation coefficient between the Sales and Profits fields. Line 1 tells Tableau that this is a script returning a number; the Python code is in lines 2 and 3; and line 5 declares the two Tableau fields to use for the correlation as inputs (in the script, these fields are referenced as _arg1 and _arg2).

LISTING 7.1

Using Python to calculate the correlation coefficient between Profit and Sales.

```
SCRIPT_REAL('
   import numpy as np
   return np.corrcoef(_arg1,_arg2)[0,1]
',
SUM([Sales]), SUM([Profit]))
```

Once you have created a calculated field with this script (see Figure 7.17), you can use it in your visualization by dragging it to the view. You use it like the Table Calculations introduced in Chapter 5.

Figure 7.17 Calculated field with Python script.

Trellis Chart with Python Script

Let's use this field to create the trellis chart shown in Figure 7.18. Start by creating a scatterplot with Profit and Sales on the two axes and with Customer ID on Detail. Then add the dimensions Region and Sub-Category to Rows and Columns, respectively. This gives you a grid with several smaller scatter plots showing how profits and sales by customer are related to each other.

Add the calculated field with the Python script to Color. Because script fields using external services behave like table calculations, you need to define which dimensions go into the calculation. In the field's context menu, select Compute Using and then Customer ID. The result should be a different color for each plot, depending on the correlation coefficient between the two measures, aggregated at the level of the customer.

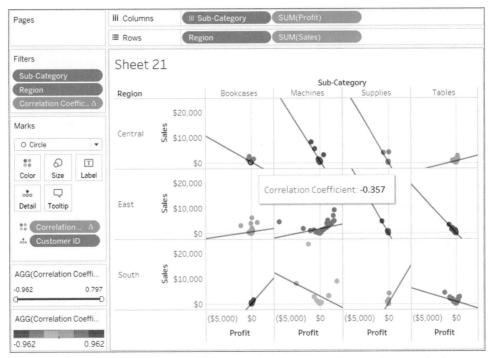

Figure 7.18 Trellis chart, with trend lines and colors according to the correlation coefficient.

TIP Trellis charts, also called small-multiple or lattice charts, are collections of similar diagrams that use the same axes and axis scales. They make it possible to compare the results from different subsections of a dataset. In Tableau, you implement trellis charts by adding different dimensions to Rows and Columns—in addition to the measures that define the axes—to break the result into smaller subsets.

Admittedly, the example of the correlation coefficient was a very simple example, and, in fact, it is not even necessary to use an external service to calculate the correlation coefficient in Tableau (a LOD Calculation with the `CORR` function or a Table Calculation with the `WINDOW_CORR` function can be used to get the same result). But I chose this example because I believe that most readers—even those with a limited background in statistics—will be able to follow what is going on here and get an impression of how powerful the external service integrations can be.

The example in the next section will be slightly more advanced. You will use a local regression to create a scatter-plot smoother. For this example, you will use R instead of Python.

R Integration

To use R in Tableau, you need an installation of R and the package RServe. RServe is the equivalent of TabPy in the case of Python, and it enables Tableau to connect to R.

If you don't have R on your machine, start by downloading it from http://www.r-project. org. Once R (or RStudio) is running, enter the following command:

```
install.packages("RServe")
```

After RServe has been successfully installed, load and run it with the following two lines:

```
library(RServe)
RServe()
```

As with Python, open the External Service Connection window in Tableau Desktop. Choose RServe in the Select An External Service menu, and set the Server and Port fields according to your RServe installation. If it runs on the same machine as Tableau Desktop, the server is `localhost`. RServe uses port 6311 by default (see Figure 7.19).

Once R is set up, you can run R scripts from within calculated fields, just as you did in the previous example with Python.

Figure 7.19 Configuring the R connection in Tableau.

Security

In many companies, a higher level of security is required than the standard R integration provides. This is because many organizations have a dedicated server for R and RServe, and the communication between Tableau and RServe is by default not encrypted, hence leaving the connection vulnerable to attacks.

Two advanced settings in the External Service Connection window can help improve security when using RServe:

Sign-In Credentials Select the Sign In With A Username And Password box, and fill in the respective fields if your RServe installation requires you to sign in with a username and password.

SSL Encryption Select Require SSL if your connection requires SSL encryption. Then click the No Custom Configuration File Specified (Click To Change) link to select an SSL certificate for the connection.

Note that SSL-encrypted connections to RServe use port 4912 (see Figure 7.20).

Example: Local Regression with R

You have already seen how density maps can help with the issue of over-plotting on maps (Chapter 6) and how moving averages can help with the interpretation of volatile line charts (Chapter 5). Locally weighted scatter-plot smoothing (abbreviated as LOESS or LOWESS) is a type of local regression similar to moving averages. In visual analytics,

Figure 7.20 Configuring a secure connection to RServe.

this is often used to trace out the pattern in dense scatter plots. The advantage over Tableau's trend line tool, mentioned earlier, is that you do not have to know the functional form of the underlying regression model beforehand (linear, polynomial, exponential, etc.). Instead, you let the data speak for itself to unearth the shape of the line.

To demonstrate this, let's take a look at the relationship between discounts and sales in the Superstore dataset. Do customers who buy more get larger discounts?

Start by creating a scatter plot with Sales on Columns, Discount on Rows, and Customer ID on Detail. The result is a very wide scatter of points, including many overlapping points in the lower-left corner of the plot. Hence it is difficult to see what the exact relationship is.

To add a LOESS smoother, start by setting up the connection to RServe, as described previously. Then create a calculated field, call it LOESS, and enter the script in Listing 7.2.

LISTING 7.2

R script for a LOESS smoother line.

```
SCRIPT_REAL("
df <- data.frame(ft=.arg1, ht=.arg2);
fit <- loess(ft ~ ht, data=df)
predict(fit)
",
SUM([Discount]),
SUM([Sales])
)
```

This script will take the sums of Sales and Discount as inputs, add them to an R data frame, use that data frame to calculate the LOESS regression line, and return the fitted values (the y-coordinates for that line).

Because this calculation returns the y-coordinates for the smoother line, you can use it to create a dual-axis chart, just as you did in Chapter 5 with the moving average line.

Add the LOESS field to the Rows shelf next to Discount, and wait for the initial calculation to finish. Then open its context menu and ensure that Compute Using is set to Customer ID.

In the same context menu, select Dual Axis. As with the previous dual-axis charts, ensure that the axes are synchronized by right-clicking the right axis and selecting Synchronize Axis. Change the chart type for the chart with the LOESS field to Line in the drop-down menu of the associated Marks card. It may not change immediately to a line chart: in recent versions of Tableau, Measure Names is automatically added to Color when creating a dual-axis chart, and that extra dimension breaks up the data. Simply drag that field off the Marks card, and the dots should be connected by a line.

You may also want to add a filter for SUM(Sales), to filter out some of the outliers on the right side of the chart, as in Figure 7.21.

As you can see, there seems to be a nonlinear relationship between the two measures. The LOESS smoother indicates that Discount increases quickly as Sales goes from 0 to around $2500. But then there seems to be a break in the pattern: Discount no longer increases much, and eventually the trend reverses as you go further to the right along the x-axis. Of course, the actual data points scatter quite widely around this line, but you now have a general idea of the underlying pattern.

TIP Python users can achieve a similar result by using the following script:

```
SCRIPT_REAL(
"
import statsmodels.api as sm
lowess = sm.nonparametric.lowess(_arg2, _arg1, frac = .75)
result = lowess.T[1].tolist()
return result
",
SUM([Sales]), SUM([Discount]))
```

Depending on how the data is originally sorted, you may have to manually specify the sort order in the Edit Table Calculation window when using this script. In this example, you will have to ensure that the data enters the calculation sorted by the sum of Sales, in ascending order, because you want the smoother line to go from left to right in the scatter plot.

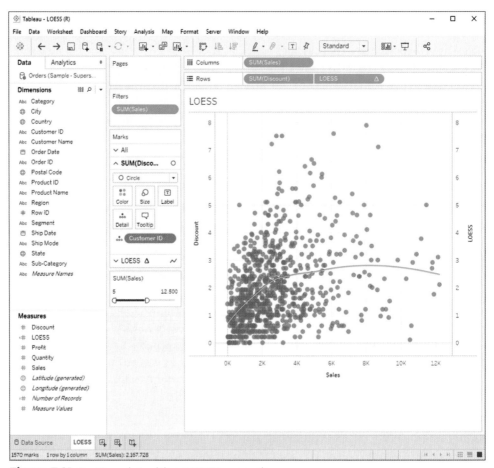

Figure 7.21 Scatter plot with a LOESS smoother.

MATLAB Integration

If you have access to your organization's MATLAB Production Server, you can also access it via calculated fields in Tableau.

Simply enter the following details in the External Service Connection window mentioned earlier: from the Select An External Service drop-down menu, select TabPy/External API. Then enter the name and the port of your MATLAB Production Server (see Figure 7.22).

As with R and Python, you enter MATLAB scripts in Tableau's calculated fields using the SCRIPT functions, and you use the fields like Table Calculations in the view.

Figure 7.22 Configuring the connection to a MATLAB Production Server.

TIP At the moment, Tableau can only connect to one external service. It is thus not possible to use different programming languages at the same time. However, you can switch between services at any time by changing the settings in the External Service Connection window.

Chapter 8

Interactive Dashboards

Dashboards provide all the important information about a topic in one view. They are a popular tool for managers and subject-matter experts alike, allowing them to stay up-to-date and to make better business decisions. Having the right dashboard available means you don't have to look for different data sources that may be distributed over multiple locations, and you have a one-stop solution to the latest data available—assuming the underlying database provides updates in (near) real time.

A dashboard in Tableau typically consists of the charts from several worksheets and other elements. They can be made interactive by linking the individual charts, so that clicking a mark in one chart changes what you see in the other charts. This adds context and allows the end user to explore the data in various ways. For instance, imagine a bar chart with product categories and a world map with sales locations. Clicking the bar of a specific category could filter the map to only show the sales of that particular product. Adding such interactivity helps bring the data alive.

Other elements can be added to a dashboard, including titles, text boxes, images, web elements, and navigation buttons.

By the end of this chapter, you will be able to:

- Combine several charts into one dashboard.
- Add interactivity with filter and highlight actions.
- Use URL actions to embed websites and allow email mailings.
- Follow an iterative process to further improve the design and usability of your dashboard.

PRELIMINARY CONSIDERATIONS

Before jumping in, it can be beneficial to pause and clarify the purpose of the dashboard. Ask yourself the following questions:

- What are you hoping to achieve with the dashboard?
- What is the intended effect?
- Who is your primary audience?
- What part of the data is most interesting for your target audience?
- Are you trying to communicate a specific point, or do you want to enable the audience to ask their own questions?
- What kinds of questions might they have?
- How can this data help your audience make better decisions?
- Are there secondary audiences or use cases that your dashboard also has to cover?

Answering these questions beforehand will help you build more effective dashboards.

That said, in practice, creating a dashboard is often an iterative process; there is no single, perfect dashboard. But with regular feedback from your target audience, you can quickly improve on a rough first design.

Making regular improvements is easily done in Tableau and also helps you get the necessary buy-in from colleagues who will use the dashboard on a day-to-day basis.

CREATING A NEW DASHBOARD

To create a dashboard in Tableau, click the New Dashboard button, which is next to the New Worksheet button that you probably have used several times by now (see Figure 8.1).

Familiarize yourself with the workspace and the Dashboard pane on the left side, as shown in Figure 8.1.

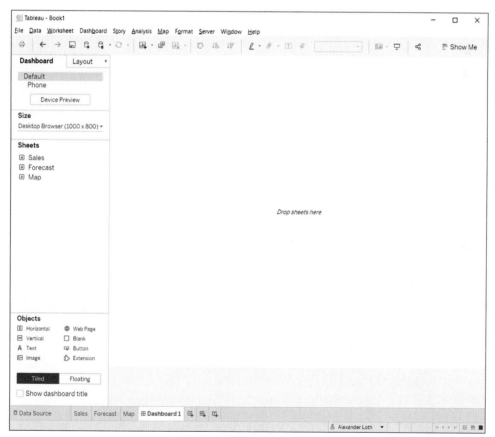

Figure 8.1 A blank dashboard.

THE DASHBOARD PANE

The Dashboard pane is essential for creating dashboards. It consists of the following sections, from top to bottom:

Figure 8.2 Defining the dashboard template size.

Device Preview   Clicking the Device Preview button will give you an idea of what the dashboard will look like on different devices, such as smart phones and tablets, and on differently sized desktop monitors. In addition, you use this tool to create alternative layouts for different screen sizes.

Size   The first step is usually to define the size of the dashboard's default layout using the Size drop-down menu. When you choose Fixed Size, you can manually define the width and height of your dashboard. You can also use common formats such as Desktop Browser (1000 x 800), shown in Figure 8.2.

Select Automatic to let the size freely vary according to the available space. Use the Range option to let the size of the dashboard vary, but only within a certain range. You can define the minimum and maximum height and width.

Automatic or range-sized dashboards have the advantage that they can make use of the full screen size. When using these options, make sure the dashboard is still usable on smaller screens. If elements are too compressed, you will have to either simplify the dashboard or create a separate layout for smaller screens using the Device Preview mentioned earlier.

Using a fixed size has the following additional advantages:

- The dashboard will look the same on each screen.
- The dashboard can load faster (due to caching).
- Floating dashboard elements are always in the same spot.

TIP Choose a size that fits well with the resolution of your colleagues' screens. The Desktop Browser (1000 x 800) setting has been found to work very well in practice.

Sheets   Probably the most important section of the Dashboard pane is the one in the center with a list of your existing worksheets that you can place on your dashboard.

Objects   The Objects section at the bottom of the Dashboard pane allows you to add additional dashboard elements. The options include Text, Image, Blank, Web Page, Button, and Extension.

Below that, you can toggle between Tiled and Floating. When Tiled is selected, sheets and dashboard objects are placed next to each other in a grid. When Floating is selected, new elements can be moved and sized independently of each other and placed on top of each other.

At the very bottom of the Dashboard pane is a check box to show the dashboard title.

TIP For beginners, it is often easier to work with Tiled layouts at first. When you use the Floating option, more work is required to size and place elements accurately. What's more, with automatic or range-sized dashboards, you have to ensure that the elements scale as intended when the size of the dashboard changes. Therefore, it is recommended that beginners use this option only in conjunction with fixed-sized dashboards.

Behind the Dashboard pane you can find the Layout pane. This has useful options for making finer adjustments to floating layout elements, but we won't touch on its features in this book.

PLACING CHARTS ON THE DASHBOARD

Both worksheets and dashboard objects can be placed on the dashboard by dragging the items from the Dashboard pane to the area labeled Drop Sheets Here.

Consider the workbook from Figure 8.1, which has three sheets: Sales, Forecast, and Map. (If you would like to follow along, take a peek ahead at Figure 8.5 and create each of the three charts in a separate sheet. You should be able to re-create these using the Superstore dataset, based on what you have learned in previous chapters.)

Starting with a blank dashboard, begin by placing the main worksheet (Sales in this case) onto the canvas. Then, add the second sheet (Forecast) in the same manner. Typically, the main sheet should sit in the top-left corner, which is where the eye tends to look first (at least, in cultures that read from left to right). So, place the second sheet below the first.

As shown in Figure 8.3, the area where the sheet will drop is shown in grey before you release the mouse button.

Tableau will group the filters and legends from all sheets on the right side of the dashboard, by placing them in a layout container. In Figure 8.3, you can see the color legend for the Profit measure.

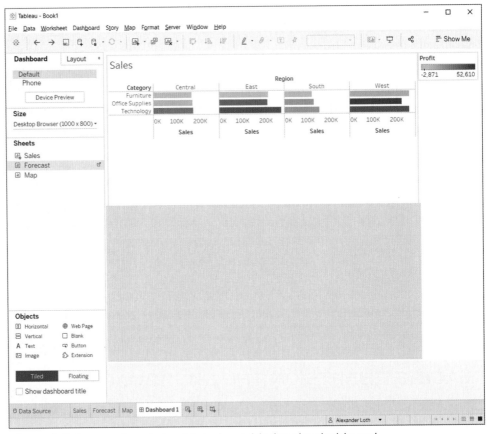

Figure 8.3 A second worksheet is being added to the dashboard.

You can also place worksheets between existing dashboard elements. When you drag a third worksheet, Map, between the container with the legend on the right and the first two sheets on the left, the dotted blue line indicates where the new sheet will appear (Figure 8.4).

TIP When you give your worksheets meaningful names, it will be easier to find the right charts when putting together a dashboard. Worksheet names can be changed by double-clicking the tabs at the bottom of the window.

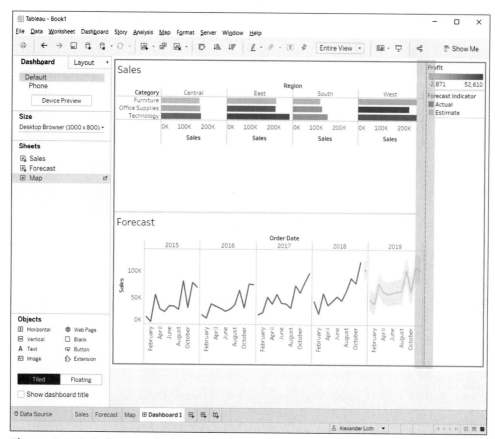

Figure 8.4 A dashed line indicates where the additional worksheet will be inserted.

In the case of this example, you will have to adjust the size of the map to make the layout of the dashboard more balanced. You do that by moving the left border of the Map container to the left, thereby giving it more space relative to the other sheets (see Figure 8.5).

DASHBOARD TITLES

The dashboard in Figure 8.5 is as yet unnamed. Right-click the Dashboard 1 tab at the bottom of the screen; in the context menu, select Rename. Then enter a name of your choosing, such as Sales Overview.

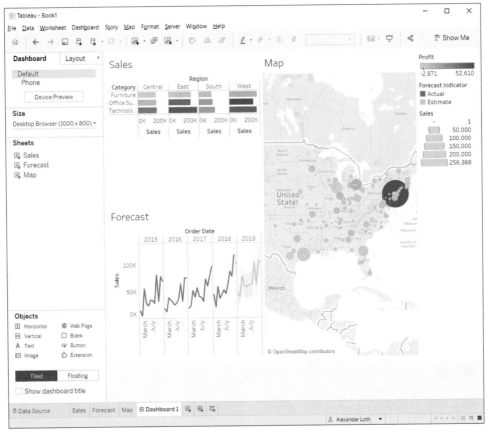

Figure 8.5 A dashboard with three charts.

Select the Show Dashboard Title option at the bottom of the Dashboard pane. As shown in Figure 8.6, the dashboard now has a proper title.

TIP Not happy with the text formatting? Double-click the title, or any other text box, to individually edit and format it.

NAVIGATION BUTTONS

By including navigation buttons, you allow end users to jump from one dashboard to another.

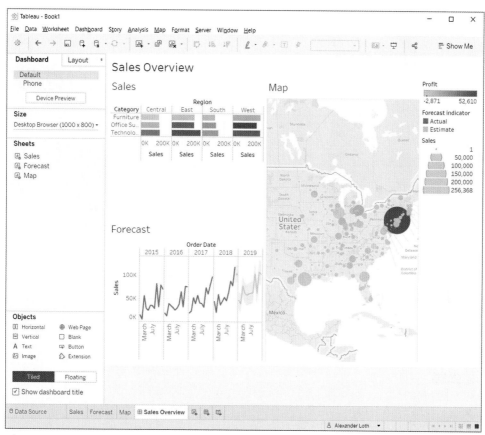

Figure 8.6 Dashboard with title.

From among the dashboard objects, find the Button item, and drag it onto your dashboard. You may have to resize the button with the mouse. In Figure 8.7, the navigation control has been placed above the color legend.

After placing the button, open its context menu and choose Edit Button. Select the target sheet in the Navigate To drop-down menu (Figure 8.8). This can be a dashboard, a worksheet, or a Story.

Optionally, you can change the image used for the button or edit the tooltip text, which tells the user what the button does when they hover over it.

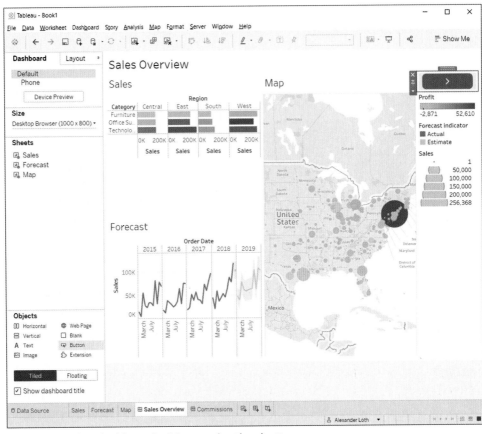

Figure 8.7 The dashboard with a navigation button.

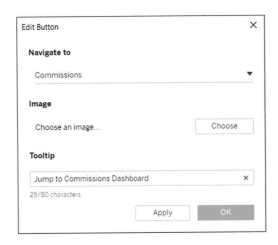

Figure 8.8 Edit Button dialog box.

TIP It makes sense to move buttons and other smaller elements out of the grid and set them to Floating, so you have better control over where to place them on the dashboard. You can do that for individual dashboard objects in the element's context menu.

DASHBOARD ACTIONS

Dashboard actions enable the end user to intuitively explore the data and better understand the connections between the different charts. Actions can be set up to filter or highlight charts, to open web content, or even to send email notifications. Advanced users can use dashboard actions creatively to implement even the most sophisticated linkages between charts. This is especially true since set actions were added in version 2018.3.

Tableau distinguishes between the following types of dashboard actions:

- **Filter actions:** Filter the target charts based on the selection in the source chart.
- **Highlight actions:** Highlight marks according to the selection in the source chart.
- **URL actions:** Open web content (and can be used to send email notifications) according to the selection in the source chart.
- **Set actions:** Change the values within a manually defined subset of your data. (Sets and set actions are beyond the scope of this book.)
- **Go-to-sheet actions:** Take the user to another sheet or dashboard, based on the selection in the source chart. (These work well in combination with navigation buttons, which can be used to take the user back to the entry dashboard.)

Filter Actions

Filter actions are a great way to link up two charts, and of all the different types of actions, they are the easiest to set up. In fact, doing so takes just two clicks. First select the sheet on your dashboard that you want to use as the source for the filter action.

Once you see the grey frame, open the small menu that appears beside it. Click the third button from the top—the one with the funnel icon, labeled Use As Filter—as shown in Figure 8.9.

Repeat the process for all sheets that you want to act as filters. To test the result, simply click one or more marks in one of the source sheets. For example, in the dashboard shown here, you could click the bar showing sales of furniture in the Central region. You can also select several marks at the same time: this works particularly well with maps,

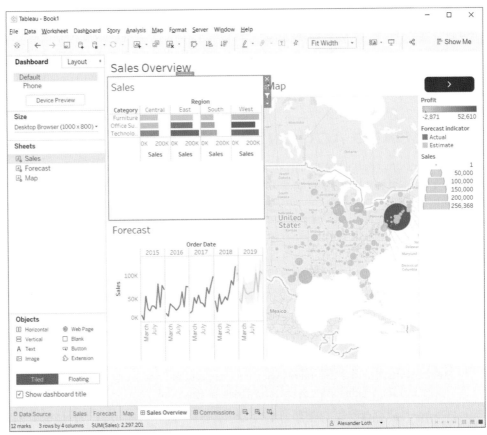

Figure 8.9 Using the top-left sheet as a filter for the other sheets.

where you can select several marks in a region by drawing a rectangle around them or by using the free-hand lasso tool. The other charts will also be filtered to only show the rows of data that underlie the selected marks in the source sheet. In Figure 8.10, they now show only data related to sales of furniture in the Central region.

To undo the filter, unselect the mark by clicking the white space on the source chart.

TIP As you can see, it is very easy to set up a filter action on a dashboard. But not every chart has to be linked to every other chart. Think carefully about which linkages make sense for your audience.

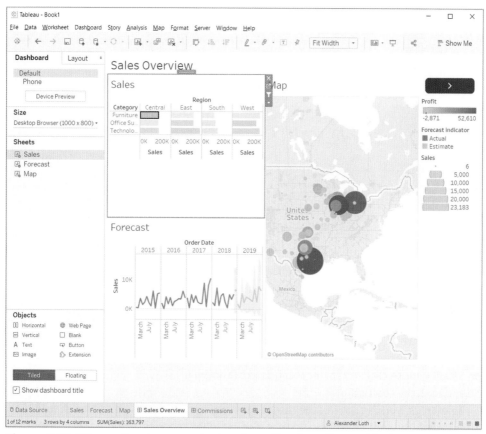

Figure 8.10 Filter action in use: only data from Furniture/Central is shown in the linked charts.

Adding and Editing Filter and Highlight Actions

By clicking the Use As Filter icon, you quickly generated a filter action. Such actions can be further adjusted and manually set up via the Actions entry in the Dashboard menu at the top of the screen. Selecting this opens the Actions window. If you have used the Use As Filter button to set up any filter actions, you will see the associated actions listed here—the addition of (Generated) to the name indicates that these were added by using the Use As Filter button. See Figure 8.11.

Select one of the entries, and click Edit to make further adjustments. Here you can also manually add dashboard actions, not just filter actions. Click Add Action to see a menu that lists the available action types (see Figure 8.12). Choose Filter or Highlight from the menu. We will touch on Go To URL in the next section.

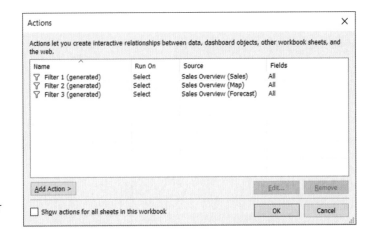

Figure 8.11 The Actions window lists all existing actions for the workbook.

After you choose a filter type, the Add Action menu opens a dialog box that lets you configure the action (see Figure 8.13), while the Edit option provides the same window to adjust existing actions.

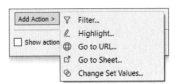

Figure 8.12 Choosing a filter.

In the Source Sheets section, you can select the sheets you intend to trigger the action. In addition, you can choose how the action will be triggered: on Hover, on Select (mouse click or tab), or Menu select (a link will be added to the tooltip).

Below that, you can specify the target: i.e. which target sheets the action should affect. For filter and set actions, you can also set what happens when the selection is cleared.

In the case of filter and highlight actions, you can specify which fields should be used to link the two charts (All Fields is the default).

TIP Target sheets don't necessarily have to be on the same dashboard. You can also link to sheets on other dashboards (within the same workbook). To do so, select the dashboard in question from the drop-down menu above the list of sheets. This can make sense, for example, if a second dashboard covers a different topic or presents a subsection of the data in more detail. Examples where I have seen this successfully implemented come from the fields of return controlling and workforce management.

Figure 8.13 Configuring a filter action.

Adding Web Content via URL Actions

It can sometimes be useful to refer to web content, such as product sheets, web forms, or even whole websites, from within your dashboard. This is where Web Page objects come in.

To set one up, drag the Web Page object from the Dashboard pane to where you would like to place it on your dashboard. See Figure 8.14.

When you release the mouse, you will be prompted to provide a URL. Enter a web address here, if you would like to have the same website displayed at all times.

But you can also use URL actions to determine the content dynamically. In that case, leave the URL field empty. Choose Actions in the Dashboard menu, and, in the Actions window, click Add Action and choose Go To URL from the menu.

Tableau shows the window to set up and edit a URL action (see Figure 8.15).

Imagine, for example, that you would like to show the Wikipedia pages for cities on a map. Give the URL action a name, such as City Information. From the list of Source Sheets, choose those that contain the dimension City. In Figure 8.15, this would be the Map sheet.

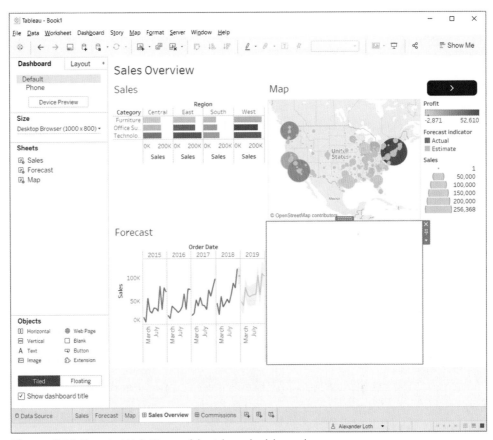

Figure 8.14 Empty Web Page object in a dashboard.

With just one URL action, it is probably best to run the action on Select. If several different actions are triggered by the same sheet, you have the option of running them from the context menu of the tooltips (choose Menu).

Most important, add the address of the website in the URL field. Use the arrow button to insert dimensions from your data that contain the entire URL or parts of it. If you had the URL for every city's Wikipedia page in your data, you would insert that field. You don't have such a field in the Superstore dataset, but you can use the fact that the URLs for most Wikipedia entries have a similar structure. So, you can use the following URL: http://en.wikipedia.org/wiki/<City>.

Here, <City> is a placeholder created when inserting the City field from the dataset. It will be replaced by the actual name of the city in question when it is selected in the source chart. Instead of using the arrow button, you can also type out the placeholder with the field name in angle brackets.

Figure 8.15 Configuring a URL action.

If your dashboard contains several Web Page objects, you can specify in the URL Target section which one to open the web content in.

TIP If your dashboard doesn't have enough space to display an entire web page, you can leave out the Web Page object and have the URL open in the web browser, instead.

To test the new URL action, click a city on the map. As shown in Figure 8.16, clicking Seattle will open the corresponding Wikipedia entry in the web element of the dashboard.

To get your creative juices flowing, here is a list of other websites that can be used in a similar manner. Note the inclusion of a placeholder in each URL:

- **Google search:** https://www.google.com/search?q=<City>

- **Google image search:** https://www.google.com/search?q=<City>&tbm=isch

- **Google Trends:** https://trends.google.com/trends/explore?q=<City>

- **Twitter search:** https://twitter.com/search?q=<City>

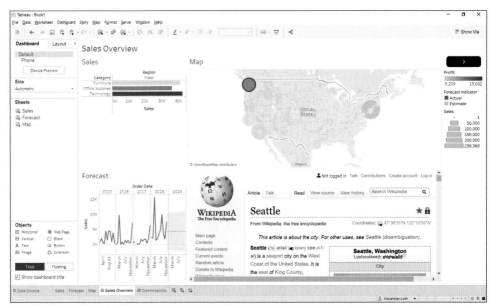

Figure 8.16 Clicking a city loads the corresponding Wikipedia entry.

Email Notifications via URL Actions

URL actions can also be used to set up email mailings from your dashboard. To do so, proceed as in the previous section, but do not add a Web Page object to the dashboard. You want the URL action to be processed by the browser, which will then open a new email in the email client (e.g. Microsoft Outlook). This happens because you are using the term `mailto:` in the URL. Specifically, the URL should look like this:

```
mailto: warehouse@mycompany.com?subject=Inventory check&body=<City>
```

If the email address also depends on the data, e.g. there is a different email address for each product manager, you can of course use a placeholder to insert that dynamically into the URL. It would look like the following example:

```
mailto:<Email address>?subject= product availability&body=<product name>
```

Note that the `subject` and `body` elements are optional and can be left out:

```
mailto:<E-Mail address>
```

TIP For this to work, you need an email client that can respond to the `mailto` URL. If you use a web email service such as Gmail, you will have to install a browser plugin first that can interpret the `mailto` function.

DASHBOARD STARTERS: TEMPLATES FOR CLOUD DATA

If you use Tableau Online in addition to Tableau Desktop, and if you work with certain cloud services, you can connect quickly to the data from these services using dashboard templates called Dashboard Starters. Tableau provides prebuilt dashboards for the following data sources: Salesforce, ServiceNow, Marketo, and Eloqua.

To create a dashboard based on one of the templates, go to the Workbooks tab in Tableau Online and click New Workbook. In the Connect To Data window, choose the rightmost tab, Dashboard Starters. See Figure 8.17.

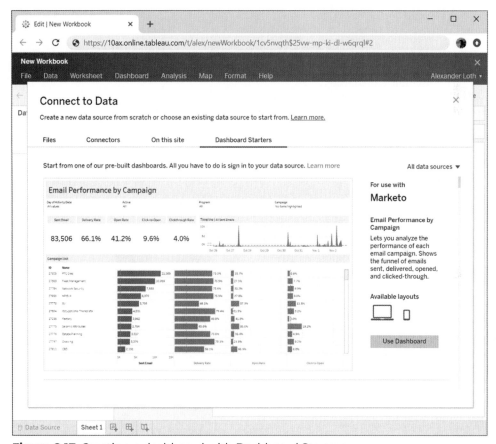

Figure 8.17 Creating a dashboard with Dashboard Starters.

Scroll through the list of templates, and choose one to associate with the data source you want to connect to. Click Use Dashboard. Finally, give the dashboard a name and define which project it will belong to.

Click Continue to create a new workbook based on this template and connect to your organization's data. If you would like to first see the dashboard with sample data, click Continue Without Signing In (see Figure 8.18).

After you click Continue, you will be asked to sign into your cloud service. You get to view a preview of the data while Tableau generates an extract.

Each Dashboard Starter contains a number of common dashboards:

- For use with Marketo:
  - Email Performance by Campaign
  - Email Performance Overview
  - Web Engagement
- For use with Eloqua:
  - Account Engagement
  - Campaign Details
  - Campaign Overview
- For use with Salesforce:
  - Account Tracking
  - Marketing Leads
  - Open Pipeline
  - Opportunity Overview
  - Opportunity Tracking
  - Quarterly Sales Results
  - Top Accounts

Figure 8.18 Dashboards can be tested with sample data by clicking Continue Without Signing In.

- For use with ServiceNow ITSM:
  - Executive Dashboard
  - Incident Report for IT Managers
  - Incident Tracker for IT Staff
  - Problem Report for IT Managers
  - Problem Tracker for IT Staff
  - Request Report for IT Managers

DASHBOARD BEST PRACTICES AND INSPIRATION

As mentioned at the beginning of the chapter, creating a dashboard is often an iterative process. After you make a first draft, you may realize, for example, that a crucial chart is missing or that the existing charts need to be tweaked in some way. It can take a few review cycles to find the optimal layout and design that the target audience finds intuitive to use.

Design Tips for Creating a Dashboard

Here are a few general tips and tricks for creating a great user experience for your audience:

Abstain From Adding Too Many Filters and Legends   Too many filters and legends can clutter the dashboard and confuse the end user. In this regard, often less is more. Therefore, don't hesitate to remove unnecessary filters and legends from your dashboard.

Arranging Filters and Legends   Group filters and legends that relate to the same content. Move them near to the charts in question or format them with the same background to make the link obvious. For the latter effect, right-click the filter or legend and choose Format Filters or Format Legends, respectively. Then, in the formatting sidebar that appears, choose a color you like from the Shading drop-down menu.

Give Guidance   If your charts are linked via dashboard actions, move the one that serves as a window into the data to the top left, and move charts that are not meant to be filtered to the bottom right. That will implicitly provide a path for your audience along which you expect them to explore the dashboard: from top left to bottom right. For instance, you could go from a high-level overview of different product categories to a more detailed chart providing the evolution over time of categories that are clicked.

Also use text fields and numbers to guide the user through the dashboard by explicitly calling out what to do, in what order (e.g. "Step 1: Select a category").

Use a Unified Color Scheme   Avoid using different color palettes. For example, if you use the orange-blue diverging color palette to show profits and losses, continue to work with this throughout your dashboard. Of course, often you will have to find a color palette that works with your organization's corporate design guidelines.

Don't Clutter Dashboards with Charts   Restrict yourself to two to four charts. If you add too many visualizations, a dashboard can look cluttered, making it confusing and more difficult for the end user to get any insights from it. Remember, you can distribute charts onto several dashboards to tell a story or to let your audience explore the data in successive steps.

This is of course not a definitive list. It contains some basic, effective tricks that I have seen can make a big impact. Also, as with many such rules, there will be times when you need to break them. The longer you work with Tableau, the more you will find out what works and what doesn't; and eventually, you will develop your own style.

NOTE If you would like to further explore the topic of good dashboard design, you can't go wrong by consulting *The Big Book of Dashboards* by Steve Wexler, Jeffrey Shaffer, and Andy Cotgreave. It has lots of great examples of beautiful, effective dashboards.

Tableau Public: A Gallery of Inspiration

Tableau Public is a free platform for sharing Tableau workbooks with the world. This gallery of vizzes, as Tableau fans call the pieces of work displayed, is a great learning resource and can be a real source of inspiration.

On the Tableau Public website, go to the Gallery tab, or go directly to https://public.tableau.com/s/gallery.

The gallery is divided into two sections (see also Figure 8.19):

- **Viz of the Day:** This features a new, noteworthy visualization every day. Use the Subscribe button to receive the Viz of the Day by email.

- **Featured:** This is a curated list of evergreen vizzes. Use the drop-down menu to find interesting visualizations related to different topics, or from organizations from different sectors.

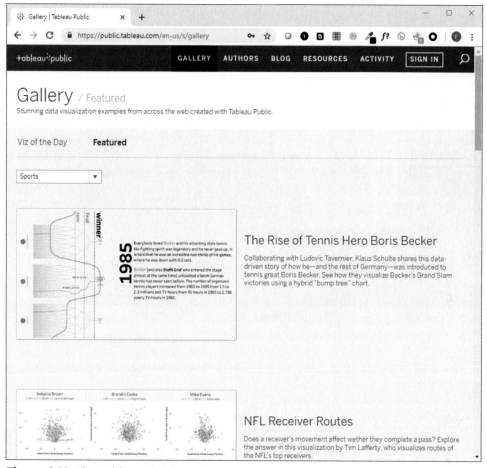

Figure 8.19 The Tableau Public gallery.

TIP Did a certain chart type catch your eye? Are you wondering how it was made in Tableau? Many authors allow you to download the underlying workbook (.twbx file). To do so, click the Download icon (1) in the toolbar at the bottom of the viz (see Figure 8.20). Then, choose the Tableau Workbook option (2). Once downloaded, you can open the workbook in Tableau Desktop and see how it was made.

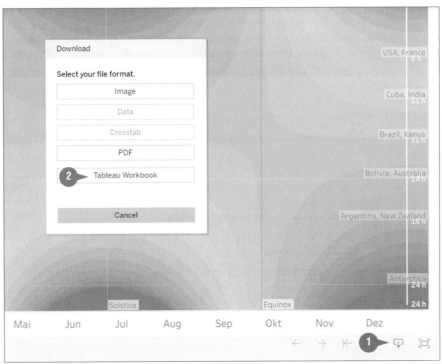

Figure 8.20 Many visualizations can be downloaded from Tableau Public.

Chapter 9

Sharing Insights with Colleagues and the World

We have talked about how to connect to data, how to visually analyze it, and how to put several charts together in the form of a dashboard. Often, the next step in the visual analytics workflow is to make the results available to an audience.

Of course, you can email your colleagues the Tableau workbook (the .twbx file). They can then open it in Tableau Desktop or in Tableau Reader. However, they need to have at least one of these tools installed on their machine, and not all organizations will allow their employees to install software as and when they need it.

Often, it is faster and easier to make your dashboards available via the web browser, using one of three Tableau products built for this purpose: Tableau Online, Tableau Server, or Tableau Public. The added benefit of sharing visualizations this way is that they can also be consumed on tablet computers and smartphones. The interactivity of the dashboards, such as the ability to set filters, is retained from Tableau Desktop.

By the end of this chapter, you will be able to:

- Publish visualizations via Tableau Online, Tableau Server, and Tableau Public.
- Work on the go with Tableau Mobile.
- Embed visualizations into websites and blogs.

PRELIMINARY CONSIDERATIONS

Before sharing anything with your colleagues or other audiences, have a final look at the following checklist:

- Can the intent of the dashboard be understood in less than 30 seconds?
- Will the end user know which questions this dashboard can help them answer?
- Is it clear what data goes into the dashboard and what the different calculated fields do?
- Will the interactivity help the end user?
- Is it clear what the different colors mean, or do they require a legend?
- Does the verbiage explain the purpose of the dashboard and help the user to navigate the charts and interactive elements?
- Did you list the data sources that were used?
- Does the dashboard's use of data comply with your country's legal regulations and your organization's guidelines around data security?

TIP Talk to your organization's data security officer if you are unsure about the use of certain types of data, such as customer data, and the resulting exposure to liability.

Once you have done the final check, you can publish your dashboard via one of the three platforms mentioned, depending on the exact audience. In detail, these platforms are as follows:

- **Tableau Server:** This is an analytical platform for organizations that either run on the organization's own servers (on-premises) or in the cloud (via AWS, Azure, or the Google Cloud Platform). Administrators can restrict access according to user type (rights management).
- **Tableau Online:** A cloud platform with functionality similar to Tableau Sever. It is hosted by Tableau and is provided as a Software-as-a-Service (SaaS) solution.
- **Tableau Public:** Often dubbed the "YouTube for data," this is an online platform for sharing data visualizations with the world. With social media components such as favoriting and following, it is used by Tableau enthusiasts to share with and learn from each other. It is also used by newsrooms and corporate communication departments to share data stories with their wider audiences.

In all three cases, published dashboards can be shared by emailing the browser link. They can also be embedded into websites or blogs. (See the section "Web Embedding.")

Another way to access a dashboard on Tableau Server or Tableau Desktop is via the Tableau Mobile app, which gives you access from on the road via your mobile devices. (See the section "Tableau Mobile.")

TABLEAU ONLINE AND TABLEAU SERVER

Organizations that use Tableau Online or Tableau Server do so because they believe large parts of their workforce require access to up-to-date data sources and dashboards. I have seen a fascinating cultural change in several companies, where the entire organization moved away from emailing each other PDF reports and Excel files and toward having conversations around up-to-date numbers accessible via insightful dashboards.

Publishing

If you have access to Tableau Server or Tableau Online, you can publish your visualizations from Tableau Desktop with just a few clicks.

The Server menu in Tableau Desktop allows you to connect to these sharing platforms (see Figure 9.1).

Clicking Publish Workbook opens a dialog box that allows you to sign in to either of the two services, as shown in Figure 9.2.

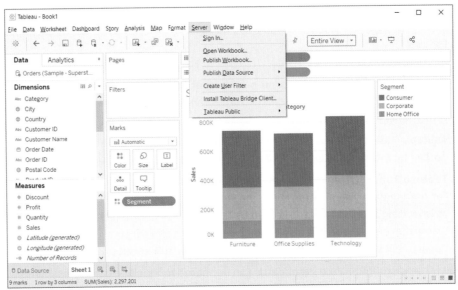

Figure 9.1 Publishing a dashboard via the Server menu.

Choose Tableau Online or the host name of your Tableau server (including the port number, if needed: for example, tableau.my.organization:8080), and click Connect.

TIP If you do not have the required license to access either Tableau Online or Tableau Server, you can try Tableau Online for free and still follow the examples in this chapter. Click Create Site in the dialog box shown in Figure 9.2 to sign up for a trial account.

If the connection was successful, you will see a window asking for your personal sign-in details (see Figure 9.3).

Enter your username and password. If your username is associated with different sites, you must also specify which one you would like to sign in on. Click Sign In. If you fail

Figure 9.2 Connecting to Tableau Online or Tableau Server.

Figure 9.3 Signing in to Tableau Server or Tableau Online.

to connect to your organization's Tableau Server or Tableau Online instance, check with your administrator to make sure your username is added and enabled.

Next, set the options necessary for the publication of your dashboard (see Figure 9.4).

Give your workbook a name and, optionally, a description. It may sound trivial, but a good description can be very useful for teammates or other colleagues who will work with this dashboard. You can organize your work according to projects. Therefore, you also need to specify which project the workbook should belong to. Additionally, you can use tags to help others find your workbook in bigger organizations.

Click Edit in the Sheets section to select which worksheets to include. If you select multiple sheets to show, you can specify how users navigate them. Select the Show Sheets As Tabs check box to provide tab-based navigation. Otherwise, users can open only one view at a time.

Select the Show Selections check box if you want a particular portion of the view to be highlighted when users open the workbook. Make your selections in Tableau Desktop before you start the publishing process.

Click Publish to complete the process and upload the workbook.

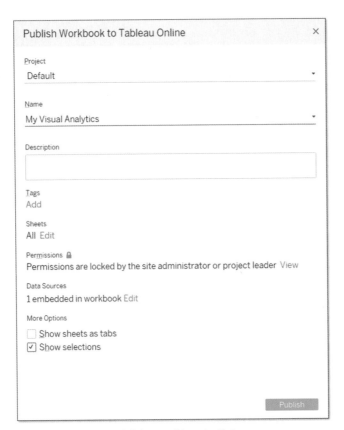

Figure 9.4 The Publish Workbook dialog.

You will now be able to find the visualization on Tableau Online or Tableau Server, and you will be able to share it with your colleagues from there.

TIP On Tableau Server and Tableau Online, workbooks can be organized into projects and subprojects and thus made available to audiences who have access rights to the different projects. Many organizations also provide sandbox projects, where people can practice Tableau. Talk to your Tableau Server or Tableau Online administrator to set up such a project.

Ask Data

Ask Data is Tableau's new natural-language interface for Tableau Server and Tableau Online. It allows you to get answers from your data by simply asking questions. Ask Data is easy to use, so casual business users and analysts alike now have an even easier way to answer data questions without having to learn how to place dimensions and measures to create charts. So, it should lower the barrier for people to interact with their data.

Ask Data is designed to work with any published data source. Simply click a data source of interest, via the data source page, and you will be directed to Ask Data (see Figure 9.5).

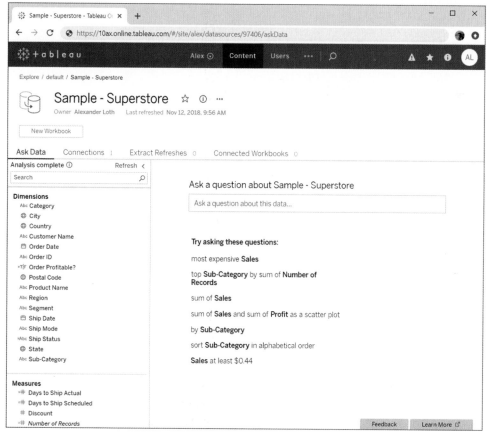

Figure 9.5 Data source with the Ask Data view in Tableau Online.

Use the Ask A Question About box to type in a question such as sum of Sales by Sub-Category. Tableau will show you a visualization to answer your question (see Figure 9.6).

Hover over any dimension or measure, and you will be presented a data preview tooltip with more insights, including the most common values or the underlying calculation (see Figure 9.7).

Tableau Mobile

The Tableau Mobile app allows you to access dashboards from your mobile device. It is available at no extra cost to Tableau Online and Tableau Server customers. To install the

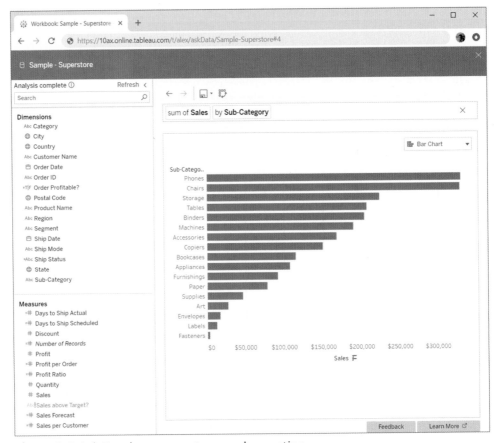

Figure 9.6 Ask Data's response to a user's question.

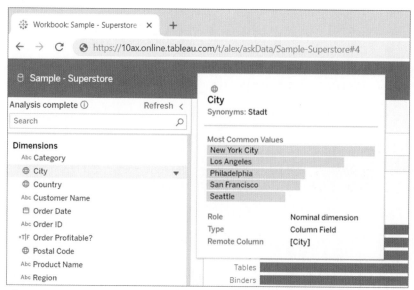

Figure 9.7 Data preview tooltip shows most common values.

app on your smartphone or tablet computer, go to the Apple App Store or the Google Play Store and search for Tableau Mobile.

Once it is installed, open the app and provide your Tableau Online or Tableau Server credentials. Figure 9.8 shows what Tableau Mobile looks like on an iPad.

NOTE This particular visualization is also accessible on Tableau Public: https://public.tableau.com/s/gallery/bitcoin-prices.

TABLEAU PUBLIC

As mentioned in Chapter 8, the Tableau Public gallery is a wonderful source for inspiration. But it can also be a very useful publishing tool, when the goal is to share a Tableau visualization with the wider world. To use this tool, you must have an account on the platform, which can be set up free of charge. Note that this is a separate account from your Tableau Online, Tableau Server, or tableau.com account.

Keep in mind that, as the name suggests, anything you publish to Tableau Public will be seen by the general public. So, ensure that you are not publishing proprietary or sensitive information. The vast majority of use cases in an organization of course do not pass that test. For those, Tableau Online and Tableau Server are the tools to use. But

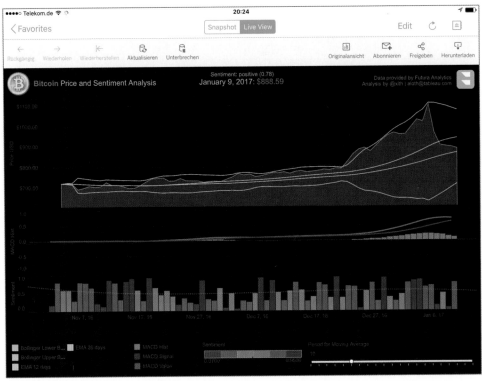

Figure 9.8 Dashboard showing Bitcoin prices, accessed through the Tableau Mobile app.

there are cases where organizations deliberately use Tableau Public to share interesting insights from non-sensitive data sources (such as public opinion surveys) with the world.

Publishing to Tableau Public

To publish a visualization from Tableau Desktop to the Tableau Public platform, open the Server menu, navigate to Tableau Public, and then select Save To Tableau Public (see Figure 9.9). Users of the free Public Edition of Tableau Desktop will find the same entry in the File menu, instead.

You will see the login screen shown in Figure 9.10.

Here, provide your Tableau Public username and password, or use the link at the bottom to sign up for a new account, if you don't have one yet.

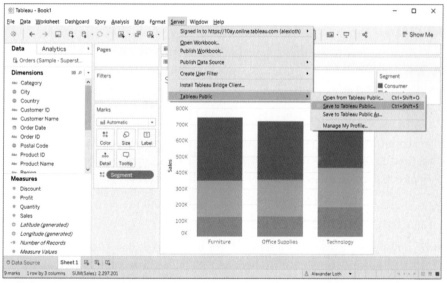

Figure 9.9 Save To Tableau Public in the Server menu of Tableau Desktop.

Figure 9.10 Sign-in dialog for Tableau Public.

TIP Save To Tableau Public will overwrite any workbook on your profile that has the same name. Often, this is exactly what you want. For example, you would do this after making further changes to a workbook in Tableau Desktop. Use Save To Tableau Public As if you want to save the workbook under a different name, instead. Choose a name for the workbook on Tableau Public, as shown in Figure 9.11.

After you confirm by clicking Save, you will see the visualization load in the browser for the first time. Scroll down on that website, and you will have the opportunity to edit some settings and provide a description for the visualization (see Figure 9.12).

Your Tableau Public Profile

Your newly published vizzes, as they are called, are shown in the gallery on your personal profile. From the profile page, you can download, delete, and hide individual visualizations. *Hiding* means visitors to your profile won't see the thumbnail; but the viz can still be seen by anyone who knows its URL.

On your profile, you can also navigate to the gallery of vizzes that you have favorited—you favorite a viz by clicking the star icon—and to lists of authors you follow and those who follow you. These social media features help you to stay on top of interesting authors and vizzes. Be sure to regularly check the Activity stream (far-right tab at the top), which is a feed of vizzes from people you follow as well as works that they favorited.

When you are logged in on http://public.tableau.com, you can always go back to your profile by clicking the profile photo in the top-right corner of the website (see Figure 9.13).

WEB EMBEDDING

Whether published via Tableau Online, Tableau Server, or Tableau Public, visualizations can be embedded into websites and blogs with a few clicks. Click the Share button in the visualization's toolbar (see Figure 9.14).

Figure 9.11 Entering a name for the new workbook on Tableau Public.

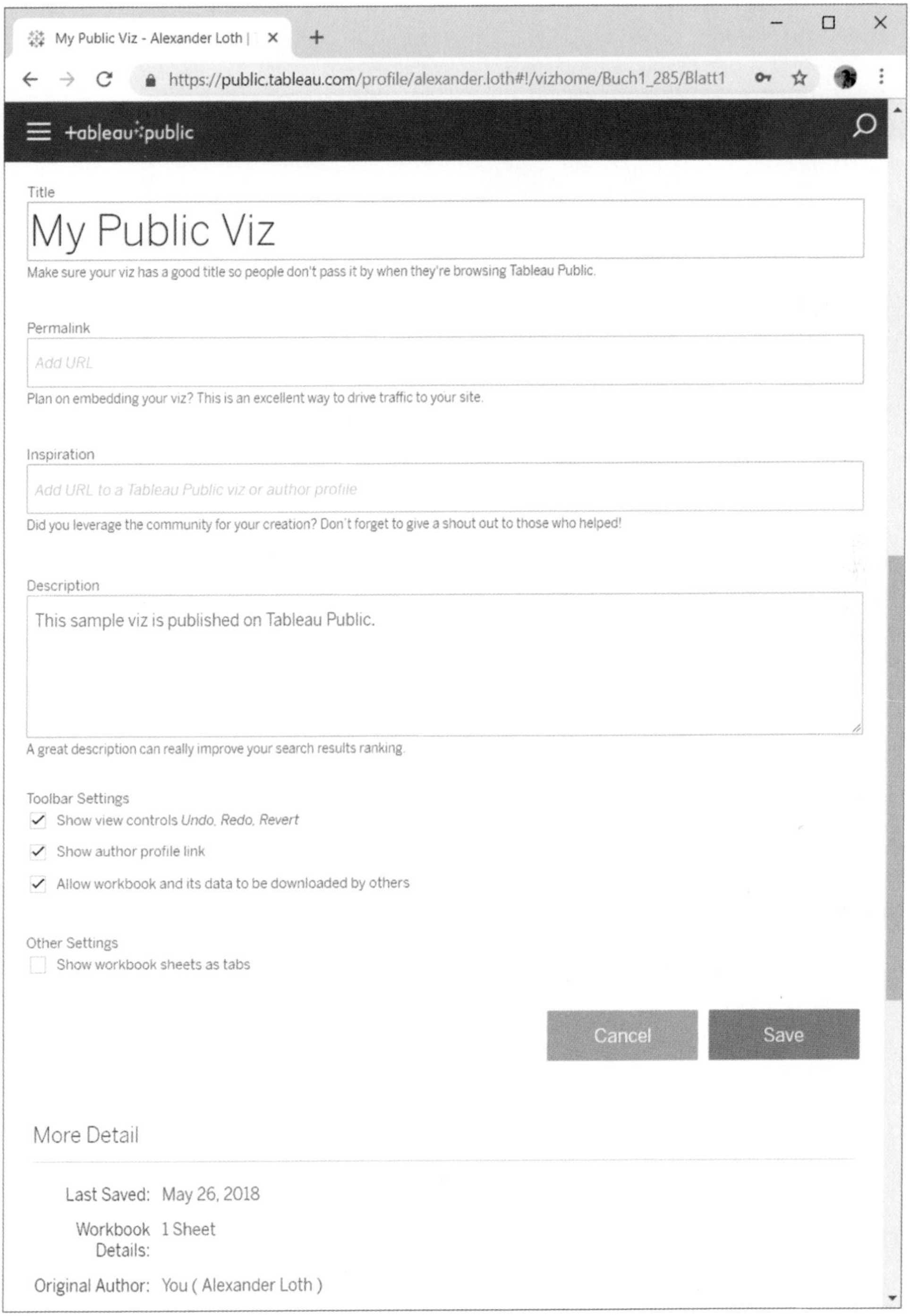

Figure 9.12 Editing the visualization's settings.

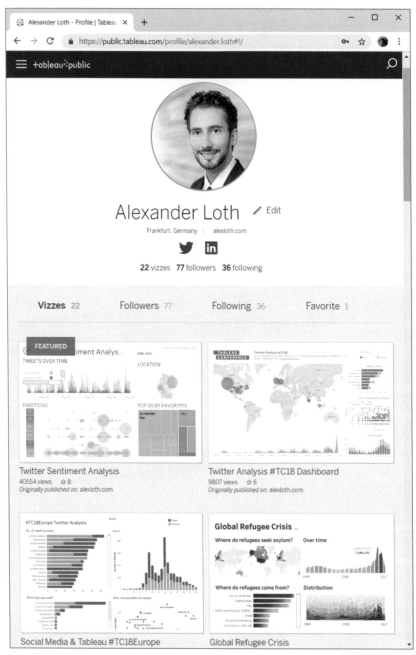

Figure 9.13 The author's Tableau Public profile.

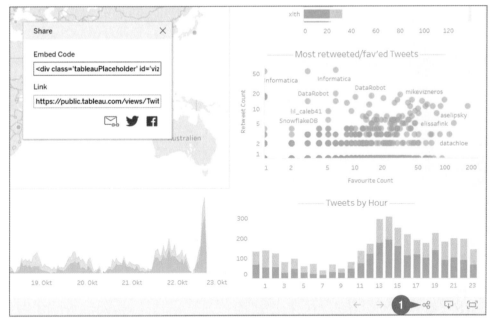

Figure 9.14 Copying the embed code via the Share menu.

Then, copy the embed code from the window that appears in the center of the viz. Finally, paste it into the HTML of your website. Embedded visualizations are fully interactive and can be overwritten with new content by saving the workbook under the same name.

It is recommended that you always use dashboards, not sheets, even if you only want to show a single chart. The reason is that you have more control over the layout, and you can make the visualization responsive so it can also be consumed from smaller screens.

For an example of an embedded visualization, see the following post on my personal blog (and also the screenshot in Figure 9.15): https://alexloth.com/2017/07/15/my-10-year-blogging-anniversary/.

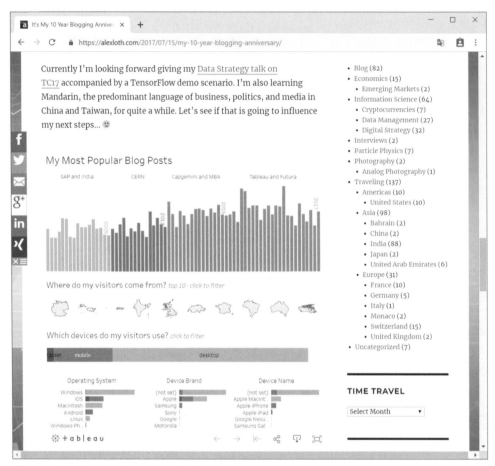

Figure 9.15 Embedded visualization.

TIP For embedding visualizations into public websites, the obvious choice is the free Tableau Public platform. But there are use cases, for example when embedding a dashboard in a corporate intranet page, where Tableau Server or Tableau Online is the better tool. This assumes your organization has the required license, of course.

Chapter 10

Data Preparation with Tableau Prep

So far, we have covered the most important aspects of creating and sharing data visualizations with Tableau, and I hope you have already been able to put some of them into practice with a dataset of your own.

However, in reality, datasets are not always as clean as the sample dataset we have used throughout this book. Further, data that is needed to answer a real-world question may be spread out over several files or databases, and the tables could be aggregated at different levels.

Thus, before you can even start to look at your data, you may need to start the visual analytics process with another step: data preparation. For this, Tableau offers a stand-alone tool called Tableau Prep, which has been on the market since April 2018.

Tableau Prep's functionality far exceeds the basic data-preparation capabilities of Tableau Desktop that you saw in Chapter 2.

With a visual approach similar to that in Tableau Desktop, Tableau Prep is intended to make data preparation accessible to business users who might not necessarily have a background in programming. The idea is that the time saved preparing data can be used more productively to visualize and analyze it.

For this reason, I thought it would be a good idea to conclude this book with an introduction to this new tool. Owners of a Tableau Creator key for Tableau Desktop can use the same license key to unlock an installation of Tableau Prep. As with Tableau Desktop, a 14-day trial is also available for Tableau Prep, for users who don't have a license yet. Simply download the installer from the following website: https://www.tableau.com/products/prep/download.

By the end of this chapter, you will be able to:

- Connect to data in Tableau Prep, and inspect and edit the data's structure.
- Clean, format, and merge different data tables.
- Create output files for use in Tableau Desktop.

CONNECTING TO DATA

The startup screen in Tableau Prep should look familiar (see Figure 10.1). As in Tableau Desktop, you have the option to start a new project by connecting to data (left panel), continue working on existing projects (center), or use a sample workbook (bottom).

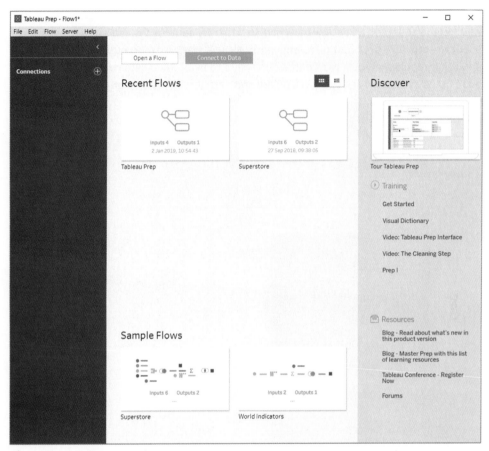

Figure 10.1 Tableau Desktop start screen.

Tableau Prep projects are called *flows*. The inspiration for this terminology will become apparent as you use the tool, but the general idea is that, for each project, you get a visual representation of how the different processing steps transform the raw data into a final output file that can be analyzed and visualized in Tableau Desktop, Tableau Server, or Tableau Online.

For this chapter, we will use sample data that is similar to the Superstore dataset we have been using. Again, we are looking at the sales numbers of a fictitious company. However, in this case, the data is a little messier. It is distributed across different files that each have their own format and structure, which is a scenario that is not at all uncommon in the real world.

There are separate files for the data from four different geographic regions (perhaps each region collected its data separately). In addition, data for the region South is distributed across files for four different years. We will start with this region.

Click the plus symbol in the Connections pane to establish a data connection. You will get a list of supported file types (To A File) and database technologies (To A Server), as shown in Figure 10.2.

The sample data is stored in CSV text files. So, select Text File, and find the correct file in the Open dialog. On a Windows machine, navigate to the following folder:

```
C:\Program Files\Tableau\Tableau Prep <version>\help\Samples\en_US\
Superstore Files
```

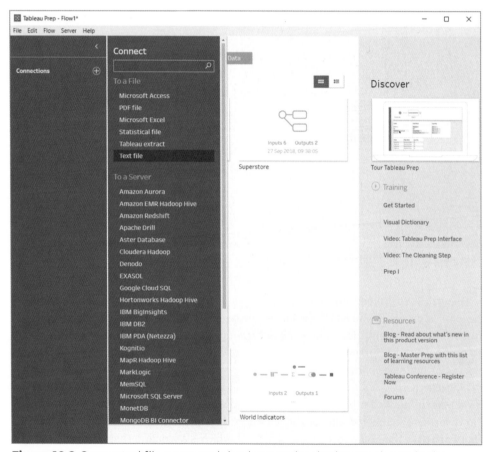

Figure 10.2 Supported file types and database technologies are shown in the Connections pane.

If you work on a Mac, choose this folder instead:

```
/Applications/Tableau Prep <version>.app/Contents/help/Samples/en_US/
Superstore Files
```

In both cases, <version> is a placeholder for the version number of Tableau Prep that you have installed, such as 2018.3.

As you can see, the folder contains several files, as well as the subfolder Orders South. Double-click this folder, and select the first file, orders_south_2015.csv, to add it to the flow (see Figure 10.3).

After connecting to the first file, you see the Tableau Prep workspace, which is divided into two main sections: the white Flow pane at the top, and the grey Input area below.

The Flow pane is similar to the data-modeling section of the Data Source tab in Tableau Desktop. Different data tables can be dropped here and placed in relation to each other. The Input pane contains different options for configuring the text file connection. There is also a table that gives you an overview of the fields contained in the data, summarizing the field name, data type, and sample values for each field (see Figure 10.4).

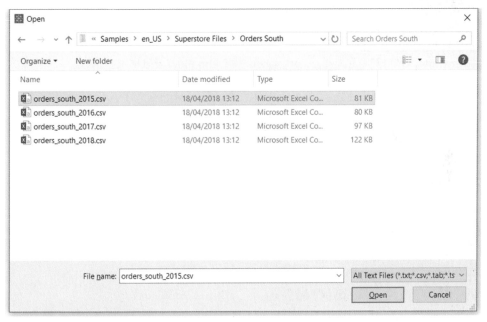

Figure 10.3 Open dialog in Tableau Prep.

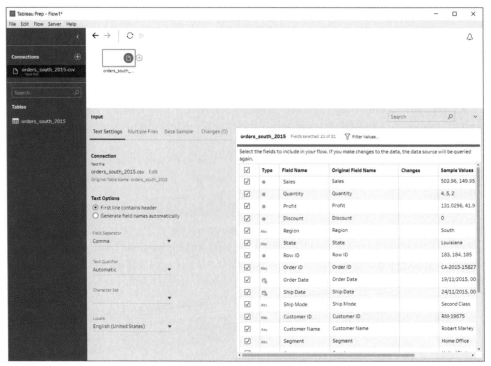

Figure 10.4 The Tableau Prep workspace with the Flow and Input areas.

NOTE As with Tableau Desktop, you are only connecting to the data, not opening it. You therefore do not have to worry about accidentally overwriting any data. Instead, the data is loaded into Tableau Prep's memory, manipulated in the tool, and then written out as a new file.

TIP If your connection contains only one data table, this table is automatically added to the flow. If it contains several sheets or tables, you can choose which one to use by dragging the table name from the Connections pane onto the Flow pane.

WILDCARD UNIONS

As you have previously seen, the subfolder South contains three more files with the same data structure; each file contains data for a different year, but they all have the same columns and column headers. You would like to integrate these into the workflow to create one table containing the data for all four years. In other words, you would like to union the data.

With just one other file or data source, you could add another connection and drag it onto the flow, as you did in Tableau Desktop in Chapter 2. You will try this approach in Tableau Prep later.

However, with multiple files, you can save time by using the wildcard union feature. More important, using wildcard unions ensures that files added to the folder in the future will automatically be included when you re-run the flow.

To do this, click the Multiple Files tab in the Input area. Choose the Wildcard Union option, as shown in Figure 10.5. At the bottom is a list of files that are included in the folder. As you can see, you now have data from the South region for all four years.

TIP As you have seen, the wildcard union feature is very useful for combining several tables of the same structure into one long table. It can find files based on similar file names, as is common with many types of data that is collected at regular intervals. For this to work, the files must be in the same folder, a subfolder, or the parent folder. Change the search criteria (Matching Pattern) until you see the files you need in the list of included files.

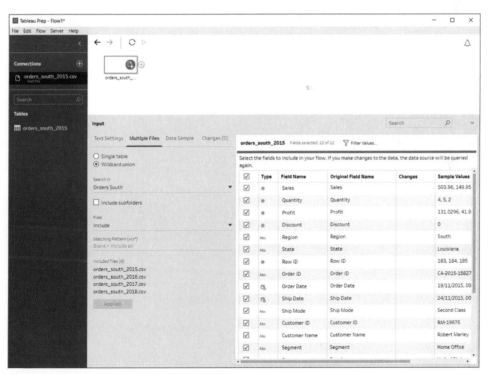

Figure 10.5 Multiple Files tab, with Wildcard Union selected.

ADDITIONAL CONNECTIONS

The files for the different years of the South region were easily combined in a union, because they are all in the same folder and have the same structure. But the files for the other regions can't be integrated as easily. For the other regions, you have one file each, and as you will see, they each have problems that you will need to take care of first.

You can select all three regions at the same time and add them to the flow as individual input steps. To do so, click the plus symbol in the Connections pane again to create another connection. As before, select Text File. Navigate to the same parent folder, and select the following two files while holding the Ctrl key (PC) or Cmd key (Mac): Orders_Central.csv and Orders_West.csv (see Figure 10.6).

Both files now appear in the Connections pane, from which you can drag them to the Flow pane. The flow now has three input steps (see Figure 10.7).

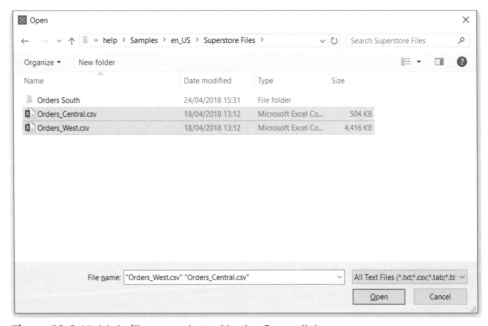

Figure 10.6 Multiple files are selected in the Open dialog.

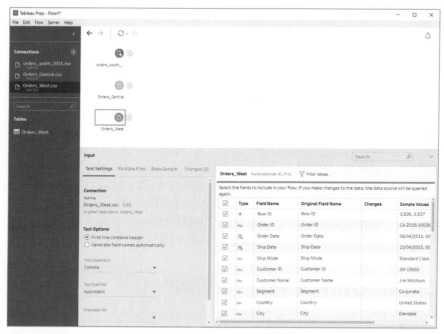

Figure 10.7 Flow with three input steps.

INSPECTING THE DATA

Your goal is, of course, to bring all the different tables together. Before you do that, you should check whether the data is in the same format and whether there are any other issues that you need to address.

By clicking each of the input steps, you can get more information about the data behind it from the summary table in the bottom panel. When you look at it, you may decide, for example, that some of the fields are superfluous and can be removed. Other fields may have been assigned the wrong data type, which is something that needs to be corrected.

TIP If you work with large datasets, Tableau Prep automatically uses only a sample of the data for the preview pane, to reduce the loading time. If a specific row from the data is not shown, you may have to adjust the sample size to see it. Go to the Data Sample tab to do that.

We have already examined the input step for orders_south_. So, you can go to the newly added input steps to check whether the data has a similar structure.

In the Flow pane, click the input step `Orders_Central`. You will notice the following disparities:

- Order date and ship date are each distributed over three separate fields: day, month, and year.
- Some fields have different data types than the corresponding fields in the `orders_south_` table.
- The `Region` field is missing.

Therefore, you need to clean up the data before you can integrate it. To do so, you will have to add cleaning steps to the flow.

But first, let's take a quick look at the last file by clicking `Orders_West` in the Flow pane. Scrolling down in the data preview table, you discover a lot of duplicate fields with the prefix `Right_`. Possibly these came about when two tables were joined at an earlier stage. In any case, you don't need to carry them through.

REMOVING UNNEEDED FIELDS

Let's start by removing those duplicate fields. In the preview table for `Orders_West`, deselect all fields that start with `Right_`, as shown in Figure 10.8.

Now these will be excluded from the flow.

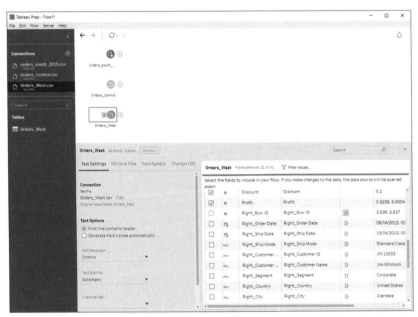

Figure 10.8 Unneeded fields can be eliminated from the flow by deselecting the check boxes.

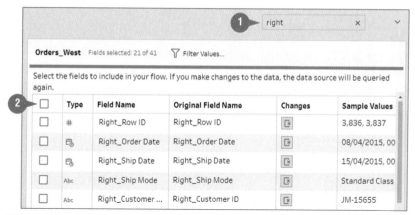

Figure 10.9 Using search to eliminate multiple fields.

TIP Use the Search field, as demonstrated in Figure 10.9, to reach the fields in question more quickly. In the example, you would type right into the search field (1). Deselecting the check box in the header row of the table (2) then deselects all fields that match the search query.

DATA CLEANING AND FORMATTING

Having investigated the structure of the data and removed any unnecessary fields, you can now shift your attention to the individual fields that require cleaning and formatting. You do that by adding another step to the flow.

Cleaning Steps and the Profile Pane

In order to remedy the issues that you noticed with the Orders_Central data, you will add a cleaning step.

In the Flow pane, choose the input step Orders_Central, click the plus symbol, and choose Add Step, as shown in Figure 10.10.

When you add such a step, the workspace changes, and you now see a detailed view into the rows of the data (see Figure 10.11).

The Profile pane opens below the Flow pane. It consists of three parts. At the top is a grey toolbar; the icons on it change depending on the selections. Beneath that are the Profile cards. These show you the field headers as well as lists of the different values contained in each field.

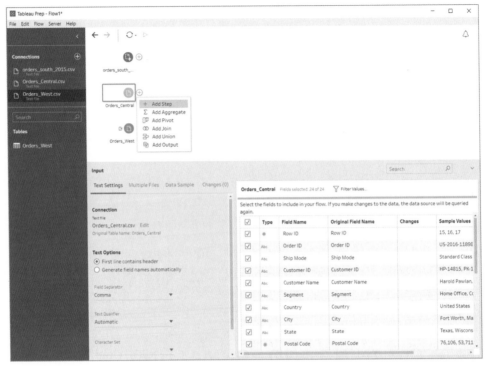

Figure 10.10 Adding a cleaning step to a flow.

The values are grouped, and you get an indication of how many data rows share a common value. This way, you can quickly see which items are the most common, how many NULL values are in each field, and whether there are any outliers that are different from the rest of the rows. This is more-detailed information that goes beyond what you learned by looking at the Input pane at the beginning. You can also address any issues right in this view.

Below the Profile cards is a preview table with the ungrouped rows of data.

TIP There is a Profile card for each field. Use the menu icon (the three dots) that appears when you hover over a card to access the cleaning tools that can be applied to the field. The other buttons allow you to change the data type, sort the data, or search for individual data values.

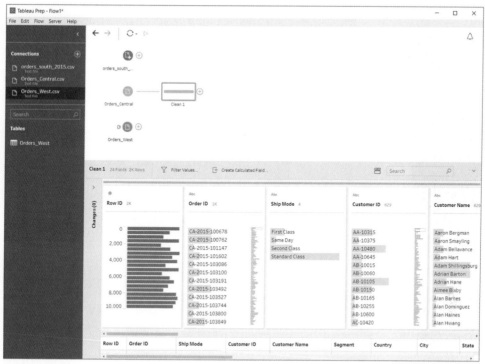

Figure 10.11 Workspace with the Profile pane.

Calculated Fields

As mentioned, the `Orders_Central` table is missing a `Region` field. You need to add this manually, so that the data can be unioned with that of the other files, which contain this field. To do this, you will create a calculated field. This is done in a similar manner and with the same syntax as in Tableau Desktop (see Chapter 4).

On the grey menu bar above the Profile cards, click Create Calculated Field. Call the calculated field `Region`, and enter "Central" into the formula field (including the quotation marks), as shown in Figure 10.12. Then click Save. This simply adds the word *Central* to each row of the dataset, which is important for distinguishing these rows from the rows of the other tables when you merge them later.

TIP When you make changes to fields and their values, these actions are shown in the Changes pane on the left of the Profile pane. Here, you can keep track of the changes made and undo individual changes. The symbol that shows what type of change was made will also be added to the cleaning step in the Flow pane and to the field's Profile card.

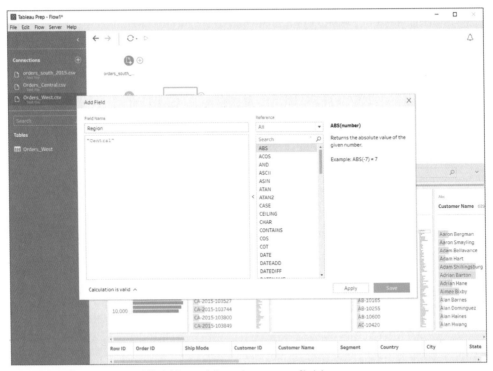

Figure 10.12 Calculated field for adding the Region field.

Next, you turn to the issue of the separate date fields for both Order Date and Ship Date. Starting with the former, you will use a calculated field to combine the fields Order Year, Order Month, and Order Day.

Click Create Calculated Field in the grey symbol bar. Call the new field Order Date, and enter the following formula, as shown in Figure 10.13; then click Save:

```
MAKEDATE([Order Year], [Order Month], [Order Day])
```

Repeat the process for the separate date fields of the shipping date. Call the new calculated field Ship Date, and enter the following formula:

```
MAKEDATE([Ship Year], [Ship Month], [Ship Day])
```

Since you now have new order and ship date fields in the data, you can remove the original fields. In Tableau Desktop, you wouldn't be able to do that, because the original fields are needed for the calculated field to work. Tableau Prep, on the other hand, works out the calculation first and then disregards the original fields.

While holding down the Ctrl or Cmd key, click the Profile cards of the different fields (Order Year, Order Month, Order Day, Ship Year, Ship Month, and Ship Day). Then open

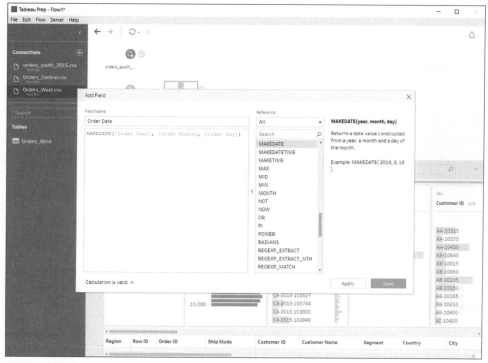

Figure 10.13 Calculated field for creating a date field.

the context menu of one of the cards, and select Remove Field (or use the Remove Fields button on the symbol bar above the Profile pane).

Built-in Cleaning Features

Another issue is that the Discounts field has the data type String (as indicated by the Abc symbol on the Profile card). This is because, in cases where no discount was applied, it was entered as None. Ideally, you would like to use this field as a measure and thus need the data type to be a number and all entries of None to be replaced by zeros.

To do this, you don't need to create any calculated fields. Instead, in the Profile card for Discounts, double-click the value None. Tableau shows you a cursor, and you can directly overwrite the value. Enter the number 0, and confirm by Pressing Enter.

Then, click the Abc symbol of the Discounts field, and change the data type from String to Number (decimal), as shown in Figure 10.14.

Renaming Cleaning Steps

In order to keep track of the changes, you can rename the cleaning step in the Flow pane. If you wish, you can also add separate steps for each of the different cleaning operations and give them even more precise names. In this case, simply double-click the current name, Clean 1, and enter Dates & Fields as shown in Figure 10.15.

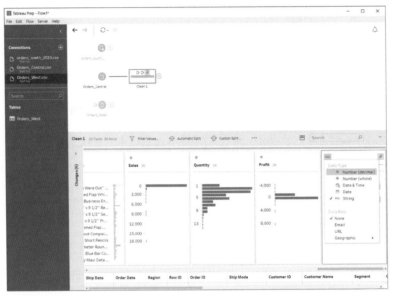

Figure 10.14 Changing the data type in the Profile pane.

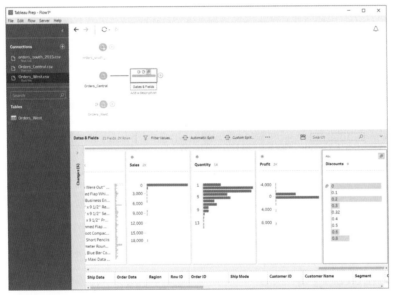

Figure 10.15 Renaming steps helps to keep track of changes.

UNIONS

Having successfully cleaned the fields, you can now merge the three different tables into one. They all contain the same fields of the same data type, and you can therefore combine them into one table that contains all the rows from each of the three regions. As before, you apply a union to achieve that.

In the Flow pane, drag the input step orders_south_ onto the cleaning step Dates & Fields, and release the mouse when it is above the New Union field (see Figure 10.16).

As you can see, a new step (Union 1) is added to the flow. To complete the process, also drop the third table (Orders_West) onto Union 1.

Now the data of all three regions is in one table. Click the union step to see the result. You should be able to see that most fields were automatically merged.

However, there are a few cases where the fields in the tables had different names, which you overlooked earlier when inspecting the data. You could have added a cleaning step to align the names. But a simpler way to fix this issue is to drag the related fields onto each other in the Profile pane. Try this by dragging Product onto Product Names, and then do the same for Discounts and Discount (see Figure 10.17).

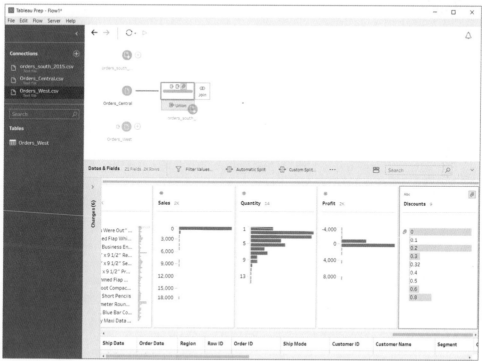

Figure 10.16 Dropping one step onto the New Union field of another step.

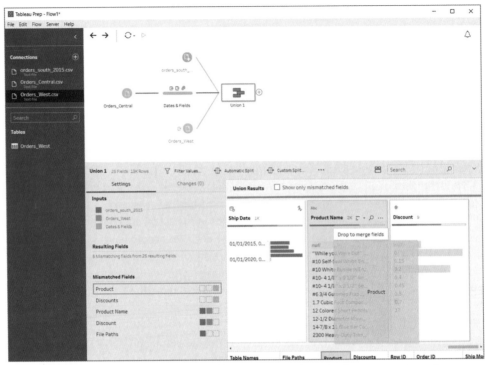

Figure 10.17 In a union, fields with different names but similar content can be manually matched by dragging them on top of each other.

TIP To more easily spot fields that were not automatically matched, click the Show Only Mismatched Fields check box above the Profile cards. This will temporarily hide all automatically matched fields.

JOINS

Let's now bring in yet another data table, one that has additional information about transactions that were recorded in your database. To be precise, it contains additional fields providing the reason that orders were returned. To bring this field into the existing table, you can use what in database language is called a *join*. But, as before, you will have to look at the data first to see if it needs any cleaning.

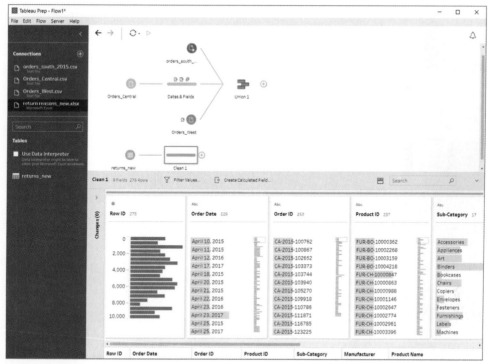

Figure 10.18 Adding an Excel file and a cleaning step to the flow.

Start by creating another connection, and look for the Excel file `return reasons_new.xlsx`. Once you have the new table on the Flow pane, use Add Step to insert a cleaning step, as shown in Figure 10.18.

Splits

The values in the field `Notes` contain superfluous spaces and also include the name of the staff member who recorded the return reason, separated from the rest of the note by a dash. It makes sense to split this into two fields: one with the reason and one with the approver's name.

First, remove the extra space characters by opening the menu on the Profile card of the `Notes` field, choosing the submenu Clean, and then choosing Trim Spaces, as shown in Figure 10.19.

Open the menu again, and select Split Values and Automatic Split. Tableau Prep now splits the field in two. In this case, it uses the dash character to identify the two parts. Give the two new fields meaningful names such as `Notes (clean)` and `Approver`.

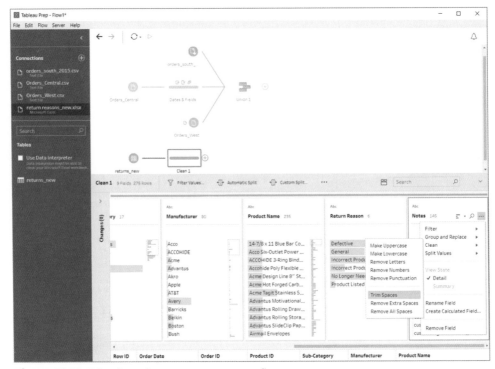

Figure 10.19 Trim function to remove superfluous spaces.

Grouping

A further issue with the Approver field is that some of the names are spelled differently. To rectify this and group similar names, open the field's context menu, select Group And Replace, and then choose Common Characters.

The Group And Replace window opens, and you see a view of the newly grouped values in the field. Click one of the names (e.g. "C Arnold") in the left table, and, on the right side of the box, you will see a list of the different spellings that have been inter-preted to mean the same thing. Here you can also manually include or exclude individual names from the selected group. If you are happy with the automatic grouping of names, you can click Done to close the window and accept the changes (see Figure 10.20).

Joining

After you have made all the necessary adjustments to the data, you can join the table with the rest of the data in the flow. To do so, drag the cleaning step Clean 1 that you

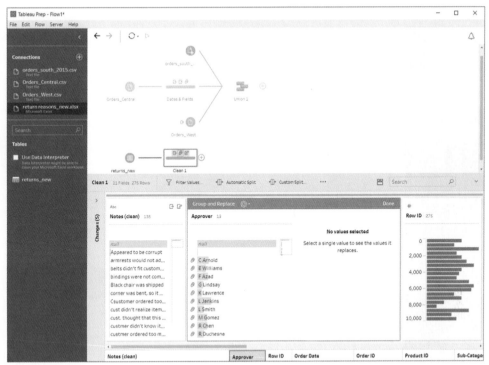

Figure 10.20 Group And Replace function for grouping different values that have the same meaning.

just worked with onto the Union 1 step. Release the mouse when it is over the New Join area.

A new join step is added to the flow, and the bottom half of the screen provides important information about the join. Here you can change the join type and define the exact clauses to be used to match the individual rows of data.

In this case, the Order ID field is the one that uniquely identifies each transaction in each of the two tables, and you can use it to define the relationship between the two. In the Applied Join Clause section, select the field Order Id on both sides of the equation sign.

The Join Type section indicates that you are starting with an Inner Join, which is the default join type in Tableau Prep. Using it, only records that appear in both tables are included. Because in this case that would restrict the data to only those records where the order was returned, change the join type to Left Join. With a left join, all the records from the left table—all recorded sales transactions in the data—are used, regardless of whether they appear in the right table (returns). To make that change, simply click the left circle of the Venn diagram icon see (Figure 10.21).

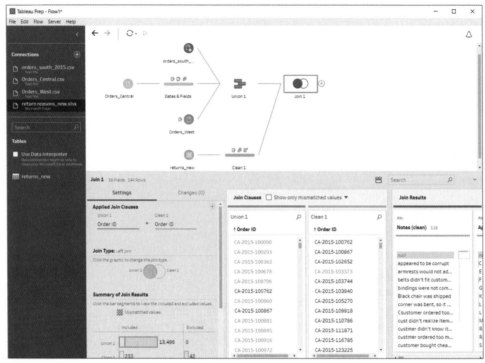

Figure 10.21 Join profile with Left Join selected.

RUNNING THE FLOW AND OUTPUTTING THE DATA

You can add as many steps to your flow as needed to clean and merge your data.

Once you are happy with the changes, you want to generate a final file that contains the cleaned data. To do that, you will need to add an output step to the flow, where you can define what type of file you would like, and then run the flow to generate the file.

NOTE You can also click any step and Preview in Tableau Desktop if you want to test the flow during development. By default, doing so generates a Hyper file where you can do some initial testing in Tableau Desktop.

Go to the far-right step in the flow, click the plus symbol, and select Add Output. You now see a preview of the final table in the Output pane below the flow (see Figure 10.22).

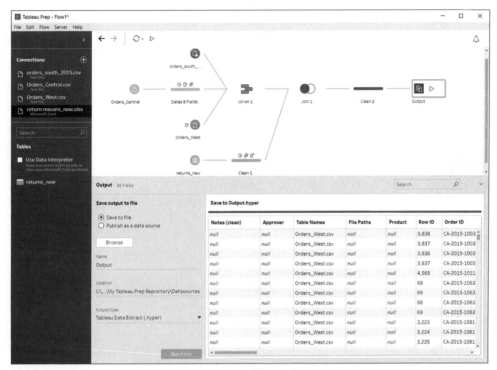

Figure 10.22 Output pane with output-to-file options.

On the left side, you can define the output type and the save location of the file. You can choose from the following file types:

- **Tableau Data Extract (.hyper):** For Tableau Desktop version 10.5 and higher
- **Tableau Data Extract (.tde):** For Tableau Desktop versions 10.0 to 10.4
- **Comma Separated Values (.csv):** Ideal if you would like to use the file in another tool, such as Excel

Finally, click the Run Flow button in the center of the output step to generate the file.

TIP Instead of Save To File, you can also choose Publish As A Data Source. This lets you upload data to Tableau Online or Tableau Server as a data source, provided, of course, you have the required access to one of the two platforms.

SAVING FLOWS

After creating the output file, you should also save the created flow so that you can re-run or edit it at a later point in time.

To save the flow, click File, click Save, and enter a name. Flow files use the TFL file format.

To open a flow, choose Open in the File menu. If new rows of data have been added to the underlying data sources, simply run the flow again to overwrite the output file with the newly processed data.

Index